THE
DUKE of
MONMOUTH
LIFE and REBELLION

For all dreamers
If you persist
Dreams can come true
This book is proof

THE
DUKE of
MONMOUTH
LIFE and REBELLION

Laura Brennan

PEN & SWORD
HISTORY

First published in Great Britain in 2018 by
PEN AND SWORD HISTORY
an imprint of
Pen and Sword Books Ltd
47 Church Street
Barnsley
South Yorkshire S70 2AS

ISBN 978 1 47389 434 1

Printed and bound in the UK by TJ International Ltd, Padstow

Typeset in Times New Roman 11/13.5 by
Aura Technology and Software Services, India

Pen & Sword Books Ltd incorporates the imprints of Pen & Sword
Archaeology, Atlas, Aviation, Battleground, Discovery,
Family History, History, Maritime, Military, Naval, Politics, Railways,
Select, Social History, Transport, True Crime, Claymore Press,
Frontline Books, Leo Cooper, Praetorian Press, Remember When,
Seaforth Publishing and Wharncliffe.

For a complete list of Pen and Sword titles please contact
Pen and Sword Books Limited
47 Church Street, Barnsley, South Yorkshire, S70 2AS, England
E-mail: enquiries@pen-and-sword.co.uk
Website: www.pen-and-sword.co.uk

Contents

Acknowledgements

No book comes into being without the support, love and encouragement from those around the author; both professional and personal. This humble first foray into authorship is no exception. These words are therefore dedicated to all those who have seen me through the process of getting this book written and produced. It is for those who have talked through ideas, encouraged me when my spirit was broken, read and commented on the drafts, assisted in the editing and proofreading. No woman is an island and I am no exception.

Firstly, I would like to thank my publisher, Pen and Sword, who have shown enough faith to help me make my dream a reality and agreed to publish this book. Thanks particularly to Jonathan Wright, Lauren Burton, Laura Hirst and Heather Williams who have been patient with my questions, as well as soothing my anxieties. This dream could not have been a reality if it had not been for Kate Bohdanowicz; thank you. Here's to hopefully more ventures into history in the future.

My thanks also extend to the tutors and professors who encouraged me during my MA at Queen Mary University of London from 2007-2009. My biggest gratitude goes to Professor Miri Rubin for inspiring and encouraging me, and to Professor John Miller for bringing James Scott, Duke of Monmouth, to my attention and starting this obsession. He supported and guided me through the dissertation that would become the basis for this book.

I owe the staff at the British Library at St Pancras my thanks for their patience and help in ordering materials, as well as helping me find items on the stacking shelves in Humanities Room 1.

To my brother, Mark Linehan, you have helped make this possible more than you know. You stepped up when I needed someone to tell me I was not a failure. You gave me back my life, you helped me restart living when all I wanted to do was turn away due to circumstances neither of us could have foreseen or controlled. You may be my little brother but you are the best man in my life. Thank you.

Thanks also go to my amazing friends: to Colin Richards - you rekindled and restored a sense of who I am and by doing so, you gave me courage to pursue my dreams, including writing this book; to Beverley Adams – thank you for your proofreading, encouragement and support. I must come to visit and you can educate me in football and butter pie; Ruth Sullivan - thank you for being amazing and understanding where others just can't and for being an Amazonian Warrior, as well as introducing me to Chris and Babs; to Julia Hopkins - London's loss is New Zealand's gain. Thank you for your love of art, history and Tosca, teamed with pictures of Lottie cat that have made me smile; to Rob Leadbeater - Darling, you have been my cheerleader, thank you. No girl could ask for more. Finally to Sarah Ursall, you inspire me, you are a wonder woman living in Derbyshire.

Finally, thank you to those who have brought this book. I hope that I will show you another side of one of the seventeenth century's most fascinating men, James Scott, Duke of Monmouth. He was far more than a royal bastard and a rebel; he was a lover, a military hero, and a man whose fate was tied to the political and religious tensions of the time.

Introduction

A university professor once told me that history is what it says in its name; it is literally humanity's story and that those of us who choose to be historians are responsible not just for the dates, facts and academic whys and wherefores, but also to the people we choose to bring back to life; we are storytellers or, as Voltaire said, 'historians are gossips who tease the dead'. This study of James Scott, Duke of Monmouth's life, endeavours to be an unbiased, human story of a man first and foremost.

James Scott, Duke of Monmouth, may have been the eldest (illegitimate) son of a monarch, but when he entered the world, his father, Charles II, was a monarch without a kingdom, and with little prospect of getting it back from Parliamentary rule. His mother, meanwhile, was a commoner with a wanton reputation. His paternal grandfather, Charles I, had recently lost his head upon a scaffold on Whitehall. Due to his illegitimate status, James had no surname of his own. He was no normal royal child; he was born on the cusp of modernity and would become a true child of the seventeenth century, encapsulating it socially, politically and religiously.

From this near hopeless start, little James would go from exile in Europe, where he lived in near poverty, to triumphantly rejoicing in his father's restoration to the thrones of England and Scotland. Monmouth would become a part of one of the most libertine royal courts within Europe. His status as a royal bastard ensured that he was able to rise within the family firm; first by being made a duke, and then by marrying into the most eligible aristocratic family in Scotland. The influences of his formative years meant that Monmouth would be his father's son when it came to matters of the opposite sex; he made a poor husband but a willing and lusty lover.

The Duke of Monmouth was also a skilled military man, with experience in the field and at sea. His ability to communicate with those of all social statuses added to his effectiveness as a military leader, as well as making him popular with the general public.

THE DUKE OF MONMOUTH: *LIFE AND REBELLION*

I hope to prove within these pages that the Duke of Monmouth was a man of his time. He was so much more than a royal bastard and a failed leader of the last rebellion upon British soil. He deserves to be remembered for more than the failed act of treason against his uncle, James II and the consequent blundered and bloody forfeit of his life on Tower Hill.

The Duke of Monmouth encapsulated the latter part of the British seventeenth century, both religiously and politically. He was active in international politics by taking part in the various conflicts within Europe through his military career. In short, Monmouth represented what made his father, Charles II' s reign great, as well as exposing where Charles was less successful. The most ironic of his father's failings that Monmouth brings to our attention, is Charles' failure in producing a legitimate son and heir. If Monmouth had been legitimate, both his father's reign as well as his own fate would have been different. History might not have given the monarchy another chance to change, evolve and modernise, and it may well not exist today.

Monmouth's story is also fascinating in that he was witness to several of Britain's biggest historical events of the seventeenth century, as well as being central to political crises, plots and eventually the rebellion that now bears his name. Among these events were the visitation of the plague (1665); the Great Fire of London (1666); the discovery of the so-called 'Popish Plot' (1678); the emergence of political parties in the form of the Whigs and Tories (1679); the start of the Exclusion Crisis (1679); the discovery of the Rye House Plot (1683) and the Monmouth Rebellion (1685).

Monmouth's story reflects the fact that seventeenth-century Britain was on the cusp of modernity in its questioning of religious beliefs and the dawn of a new scientific age, as well as raising questions about the link between church and state. Restoration Britain was still feeling the effects of the Tudor Reformation from the previous century and, unsurprisingly, feared a reprise of Mary Tudor's 'bloody' Counter-Reformation.

These social and religious complexities were confused further as the country was still dealing with the memory of a bloody and divisive Civil War, which had its own complexities of state and religion. That was followed by a restrictive Commonwealth, under the hard-lined and puritanical Oliver Cromwell. Cromwell replaced the inherited tyranny of absolutist monarchy for the even more domineering rule of military totalitarianism. Fear about rule, religion and the role God has within the state in Restoration Britain is easily understood when you explore these ideas further.

INTRODUCTION

Monmouth, therefore, is an important, historical figure from this emerging modernism of the late seventeenth century. He personified this period in a charming and dashing form. He was also a victim of his time, which combined with the poor choices he made in the latter part of his life. But most importantly of all, Monmouth was a son, a father, a husband, a lover and a man with all the faults any man has. He lived his life fully and when faced with the consequences of his actions, he died as he lived, bravely and for what he believed in. Monmouth was influenced by men who had the foresight to want a more democratic monarchy, which would work with, rather than against, parliament for the good of the whole country. He also hoped to try and preserve a Protestant Britain, which to a modern reader may seem prejudiced within a multi-faith society. This is why James, Duke of Monmouth, deserves to be examined and remembered as a man of the seventeenth century and not merely a rebel and a traitor.

Author's note:
Throughout this book, original currencies and/or monetary values have been used and the decision has been taken not to provide any modern equivalents. Providing such values are extremely problematic, due to the numerous factors and variables which need to be taken into account. However, should the reader wish to discover more about the changing values of money, the Bank of England online calculator is an excellent resource.

Chapter 1

Why the King Lost his Head

Although Monmouth had not even been born at the beginning of the English Civil Wars in 1642, they are important to his story as their aftermath still affected the political, religious and social environments during the Restoration, and as a consequence, therefore, his eventual fate. Key themes that are at the root of the causes of the English Civil Wars were the fear of autocratic rule of a monarch and the dogma of the Divine Rights of Kings, as well as fear of Catholic influence of the monarch and the potential conversion of the nation back to Roman Catholicism.

The climax of the Civil Wars resulted in the execution of Charles I. After the regicide, Britain was then governed by a parliamentary republic that became known as the Commonwealth. The Commonwealth was overseen by Oliver Cromwell, under the title of Lord Protector.

Under the Commonwealth, Cromwell and his government were mainly made up of men who were Puritan Protestants and as a result, the Church of England became suppressed during what we now know as the Interregnum years (a de facto republic with puritan morals that formed the backbone of everyday life, as well as national politics). This meant that at the Restoration in 1660, the Anglican Bishops and the beginnings of the Court party would ensure that the nonconformist Protestants, such as Puritans, were suppressed. Catholics were also singled out and the result was that fear of both Catholics and non-reformists was common. These fears meant that Monmouth was seen as a good Anglican Protestant and thus a practical possible alternative to his Catholic uncle, James, Duke of York.

The English Civil Wars of the seventeenth century were unlike the previous periods of civil unrest and conflict, such as the struggle for the throne between Matilda and Stephen in the thirteenth century, or the infamous and bitter battles between the two royal Plantagenet houses; the red rose of Lancaster and their rival, the white rose of York, which have become known to history as the Wars of the Roses. The conflicting ideas were centred around *how* the monarch and parliament were going to rule the nations of England, Ireland and Scotland together, rather than *who* should govern the nations. At the time, Wales was a principality of England (as indeed it is still), and Ireland was considered to fall under the crown of England. Scotland had only united with England upon the death of Queen Elizabeth I in 1603. When Elizabeth died, the new king, James I, had been King James VI of Scotland since 1567, but now the two rival nations were finally united by a single monarch, although the union was not formalised in law until the reign of Queen Anne in 1707. The contentious issues of how a monarch and parliament should govern continued after the fall of the Commonwealth and into the reign of Charles II. These unresolved issues would affect all of the political, social and religious squabbles and hang ups that followed.

It is incorrect to refer to the period of 1642-1651 as the English Civil War, as during this time there were three separate conflicts fought between two sides; the crown and parliament. These conflicts were also fought in England, Ireland and Scotland. So, referring to these conflicts collectively as the English Civil War (singular) in terms of conflict and nation is wrong and misleading. The first of these wars took place from 1642-1646, when Charles I clashed with his parliament. Two years of peace followed before once again, from 1648-1649, Charles found himself at loggerheads with his parliament. This ended with parliament winning the war and Charles losing the crown, and his head, in January 1649. The conflict would later resume in 1649 despite the king's execution. This contention was between Charles II fighting for his father's lost crown against the men (the Parliamentarians), who had killed his father on Whitehall. After chasing each other around the country, the war ended at the Battle of Worcester and Charles II fled to Europe for the duration of the Commonwealth of Britain under Cromwell.

Although Charles II wanted a religiously tolerant society, the Anglicans had become resentful of the oppression they had faced during the Commonwealth years. Following the Restoration, they sought to eliminate anyone they saw as a threat to their regained religious freedom, regardless of whether the threat came from a Protestant or Catholic. This goes some way to explain the religious and political objections towards the Catholic Duke of York as the potential heir to the throne.

Charles I was not the first monarch from the royal house of Stuart to have struggled with his parliament; he was just unlucky in his judgment. He failed to understand or learn how to manage and manipulate them successfully. When his father, James I, inherited the throne from Elizabeth, he had already been King of Scotland for thirty-six years. As Elizabeth had rarely called her parliament during her reign, James' parliament had different hopes when he replaced her as king. James had managed to tame the Scottish parliament in 1583 and was not prepared to be dominated by the bigger legislative body in Westminster. He fully believed that he was put on the throne to rule by God's good grace and that he had a divine right to be king. Just like his son and grandson after him, James I managed his parliament by dissolving it when he was unhappy with the way that they attempted to control him. And just as in the reigns of Charles I and Charles II, the crux of this power held by parliament was money. They held the power to control funds for the royal coffers through taxation legislation. James I's reign also haunted that of his grandson Charles II. This was because it was during the early part of James' rule that the group of Catholic fundamentalists involved in the Gunpowder Plot tried to blow up the Houses of Parliament and eliminate the new Scottish Protestant monarch and the whole of his Protestant ruling class. This historical event was used to fuel the public's fear of Catholicism during the Restoration.

Charles I therefore had no template to show him how to be a king. He merely followed the example set by his father, as well as inheriting his father's belief in the Divine Rights of Kings and bitterly resenting parliament for keeping him on a short leash, financially. His relationship with his Protestant government was probably not helped by his choice of a Catholic wife, Henrietta Maria. The queen consort was the daughter of Marie de' Medici, famous throughout Europe as a powerful and influential regent to her son, Louis XIII of France. Henrietta Maria would have been seen as a dangerous influence upon the king as she would have seen first-hand the power and success of an absolutist monarchy in France. As the daughter of a Medici, she certainly had a fierce Italian temperament and expressed strong opinions with her children and her husband on both issues of state and religion. Charles' marriage to Henrietta Maria would have also caused parliament concern because they would have disliked England being joined in marriage to her old rival, France.

One of the main causes of the Civil Wars was because Charles I refused to call parliament for eleven years from 1629 until 1640. This was because he was so frustrated by their attempts to control him. As they held the purse strings to the royal treasury, Charles was required to find ways to cut his costs and to economise. One of the ways he did this was by ending British involvement in the Thirty Years War with Catholic European rivals Spain and France. War was expensive and no doubt this would have pleased his French wife Henrietta Maria as well. By pulling out of the war, Charles was abandoning fellow Protestant nations, Denmark and the Dutch Republic, and this would also have made Parliament nervous.

Charles also made himself unpopular among his subjects by trying to impose a ship tax upon counties with no coastline. The reason Charles asked his inland subjects to pay this additional tax was to help pay for the upkeep of the Royal Navy's defence of the whole nation. Technically, Charles had found a law that had been allowed to lapse over the decades and all he tried to do was reinforce it, for his own benefit, without any parliamentary backing. The lack of parliamentary support led to some subjects refusing to pay this re-imposed tax. Refusal to pay resulted with the non-payers being brought before a court, where they were fined for their trouble as well as taxed. Charles did not win friends or support from his subjects through this endeavour and he was still no better off for his attempt.

Anglican Protestantism, adopted by the church within England after the Reformation under King Henry VIII, was always closer in practice to the traditional Catholic mass than any of the other more extreme forms of Protestantism, such as Lutheranism. Due to the fact that Charles I had ruled without the intervention of parliament, this came to be viewed by some to have brought the Anglican communion closer to absolutist monarchy and by association, Roman Catholicism. The king also changed the Anglican services with the help and encouragement from the Archbishop of Canterbury, William Laud, further causing worry and fear that Charles was trying to reconvert England back to Rome. Once again, these fears and their after effects were still being felt well into the reign of his son. At the Restoration there were men serving in parliament who had lived through the Civil Wars and Commonwealth period and felt they had a just cause to fear a Catholic king inheriting the throne.

Charles' attempt to press religious reform in Scotland would bring about his political downfall. Scotland had a more episcopal form of Protestantism, meaning that their church, also known as the Kirk, was overseen by bishoprics rather than the monarch, as is still the case today. Charles desired that all his kingdoms within Britain should follow a new High Anglican version of the Common Book of Prayer during their masses. Scotland, however, was resistant to this change in doctrine. The Scottish Reformation had happened when both England and Scotland had separate monarchies. The Scottish church's form of Protestantism was always more akin to northern European reformist Protestants, rather than the 'softer' Anglican communion. Charles I was effectively trying to reform their church again and understandably, they resisted. This resistance reached breaking point in Edinburgh, when resistance turned into violence outside St Giles' Cathedral in the summer of 1638.

The unrest that started outside St Giles' spread throughout Scotland in protest to these new doctrinal changes. Eventually, in early 1639, Charles went to Scotland in the hope of repressing the violence. While he was there, the two sides came to an agreement known as the Pacification of Berwick. However, the peace brokered through the treaty did not last long, as just over a year later, in the summertime of 1640, fresh riots broke out. This time Charles was beaten by the Scots who came over the border and occupied Newcastle. To make things worse for Charles, he had to pay Scotland reparations to cover their war expenses. This would break the royal treasury and due to his arrogance in trying to dominate the Scottish Church, Charles found himself forced to recall parliament for the first time in eleven years.

This parliament has become known as the 'Short Parliament'. His motive for recalling it was to obtain more money to fund another campaign in Scotland. However, the members of parliament, after being silenced for so long, were not just going to give the king what he wanted. The majority of the House of Commons, led by John Pym (political parties were yet to be established), decided to use this time not to discuss Scotland, but to make plain their unhappiness towards the behaviour of Charles himself. Charles took this as an act of *lèse-majesté*, literally seeing it as a criminal act against himself as the monarch and as such, decided to dissolve parliament, despite not getting what he wanted from them. The parliamentary session had only lasted three weeks.

When you understand how Charles II's father had behaved prior to and during the Civil Wars, it becomes quite understandable why many within parliament, after the Restoration, feared that Charles II may take after his father. This may have been why Charles attempted to create religious tolerance within the early part of his reign, and why he waited until his deathbed to convert to Catholicism, as it was associated with absolute rule.

Having failed to get support politically or financially from his parliament, Charles doggedly attacked Scotland again for not bending to his demand and adopting the new Anglican Book of Common Prayer. This rash and egotistical assault on Scotland meant that a large part of the north of England was invaded and held by the Scottish. For a man with so little capital, Charles found himself as the king of both Scotland and England paying for both the English and the Scottish armies while they were on English soil. On top of that cost, Charles was also paying a whopping £850 per day to keep the Scots from invading any further in to England.

In an attempt to try and resolve the situation with the Scots, the king recalled Thomas Wentworth, 1st Earl of Strafford, from his post of Lord Deputy of Ireland. Strafford had used his diplomatic skills in Ireland and managed to generate tax from the Catholic gentry by promising them religious toleration. Charles was hoping that he could also achieve this in Scotland with the Kirk. Unfortunately, not even the diplomatic charm of Strafford could resolve the hornets' nest of trouble the king had provoked in Scotland.

Although Charles had dismissed parliament, he still consulted the House of Lords, which without the Commons is known as *Magnum Concilium*. The Lords, however, advised the reluctant king that he needed to recall a full parliament in this matter. If Charles had disliked his previous short-lived parliament, then he was not going to like his next one much either. This parliamentary session has, perhaps not unexpectedly, become known as the 'Long Parliament'.

Charles called parliament with the intention of obtaining money to finish his war against the Scottish Kirk and its rebellious supporters. However, the Commons decided to launch the new parliamentary session by criticising Charles for his behaviour rather than helping him and were angry and frustrated at the fact that they had been neglected for so long. This parliament would become known as the 'eleven year tyranny', and was to be subsequently recalled and dismissed at Charles' whim. Parliament resolved to change this by pushing through new laws that stated the parliamentary body should be called at least every three years and if the monarch failed to call his government, then they, the parliament, should still meet. This would become law in May 1641, with the passage of the Triennial Act. It became illegal for the monarch to raise taxes without their knowledge or consent and another safeguard ensured that he was forced to recall parliament frequently. This change in the law explains why Charles II had to find money through other means to allow himself not to have to recall parliament at the end of his reign.

Parliament then proceeded to punish Charles in the cruelest way possible; by attacking one of his biggest allies, the Earl of Strafford. Strafford had helped Charles to be independent of parliament, as he had raised taxes in Ireland so that Charles was less reliant upon them. Strafford consequently found his loyalty to the king rewarded by facing capital charges of High Treason. A Bill of Attainder was created, meaning that no evidence was needed to justify his guilt, only the agreement of the king, without Strafford having to undergo a trial for his alleged crimes. Charles struggled to follow through parliament's Act of Attainder, because Strafford had only ever been loyal and obedient to him. The Lords, of whom Strafford was one, of course, felt compelled to pass and comply with the Attainder after the Commons voted in April 1641, with 204 in favour of his guilt. Only 59 MPs voted against, while 250 cowardly abstained from voting altogether. Charles eventually signed Strafford's death warrant in May 1641, but only after Strafford himself wrote to the king asking him to sign it. On 12 May he was beheaded.

With the execution of the Earl of Strafford, both the crown and parliament were hoping to have resolved many of the differences between them and avoid the slide into civil conflict. However, Charles' resentment and animosity towards his parliament grew, while the Commons' suspicion of the king increased as they feared he would impose High Anglican Protestantism on the whole nation, with no consideration for other denominations. They also feared that Charles would use the army to enforce his will. This uneasiness would cause the Irish Catholics to fear for their religious freedom to practise their faith, and for Ireland to slip into unrest.

Charles knew he had lost his parliament in January 1642 when the Speaker of the House, William Lenthall said, 'May it please your Majesty, I have neither eyes to see or tongue to speak in this place but as the House is pleased to direct me, whose servant I am.' In saying this, Lenthall was declaring that he was parliament's man now, and he was ruled by them, rather than the king. Civil war at this point was only a matter of time.

In terms of religion, Republicans were either Presbyterian or Independent Protestants, the most common form of which was Puritanism. The Republicans all had a political desire to see that England, Ireland, Scotland and Wales were governed under a parliamentary system, instead of under the rule of a monarch. Many would have been happy to have a constitutional monarchy like we have today, with parliament and the monarch working together. Leading Parliamentarians who sought to work with the monarchy rather than abolish it were Thomas Fairfax; Edward Montague, 2nd Earl of Manchester; and Robert Devereux, 3rd Earl of Essex[1]. In the cases of Manchester and Essex, both men were part of the aristocracy and may have feared what would have happened to them if the crown fell. Therefore, it was better for them to have a monarchy that parliament could work alongside.

Probably the most prominent and well known Parliamentarian was Oliver Cromwell, who would go on to become the Lord Protector during the Commonwealth. Cromwell would be king in all but name and he even lived in former royal households such as Hampton Court Palace. No political provision was made for what would happen upon the Lord Protector's death and subsequently Richard Cromwell inherited the role following his father's death, just as the crown is inherited in a monarchy.

Within the Parliamentarian movement were other smaller factions with their own agendas, political beliefs and religious preferences. These included the groups known as Levellers and Diggers.

The Levellers believed in Popular Sovereignty, the belief that the populace should choose their rulers (both monarch and parliament), that there should be universal suffrage, equality before the law of the land and that there should be religious freedom and tolerance. Many of these ideas are seen as basic human rights in the twenty-first century, however, in the early seventeenth century they were seen as radical and dangerous, both politically and socially. People had their places within society and such ideas would allow people to be all the same, regardless of what their place was in the social structure, their gender or religious background. All of these parameters had previously kept society in check. The perceived leaders of the Levellers were John Lilburne, Richard Overton and William Walwyn.

Diggers were more extreme in their political beliefs. They were politically socialist and verging on communist in their political dogma. They believed that land did not belong to one lord, but to the people who worked it. The Diggers set up communities and farmed communally in Cobham, Surrey, Wellingborough, Northamptonshire, and Iver, Buckinghamshire.

The Parliamentarians were therefore much harder to define politically. They were unhappy politically but were not united in their political and social goals. As a group, even after they won the Civil Wars, there were too many conflicting views for there to be political, religious and social harmony.

On the Royalist side, the term 'Cavalier' was initially a derogatory term used to refer to the supporters of Charles I in the run up to and during the Civil Wars. Many of his supporters followed the Prince of Wales into exile for the duration of the Commonwealth's rule in England. Among the Cavalier followers that remained loyal to the crown was Edward Hyde, who later became the Earl of Clarendon.

Later, the royal supporters would adopt the term to describe themselves. The Cavaliers could be recognised by their courtly flamboyant dress style, which was adorned with lace, ribbon and silks, while their hats often sported exotic feathers. Dress did not just reveal their political loyalty to the monarch but also their social status, as lace and ribbon were the seventeenth century equivalent of high-end designer brand names and were expensive luxuries.

Politically, the Cavaliers were the embryonic start of the Court faction which would later evolve and transform into the Tory Party. Religiously, they were Anglican Protestant and Catholic, although not necessarily openly practising. It was the Catholic element and its close proximity to the crown that would sow the seeds of fear about absolute monarchy during the Restoration, encourage the policy of Exclusion, and consequently the fate of the Duke of Monmouth.

On the evening of 10 January 1642, Charles I realised that it was unsafe for him to remain in London. He left the city with Henrietta Maria and his three eldest children, including the princes Charles and James. It was a spur of the moment act that left the royal household little time to prepare. They would first stay in Hampton Court Palace, before moving on to Windsor Castle. The rift between sovereign and his parliament had widened. A letter from Thomas Wiseman to Sir John Pennington on 6 January states 'The House has occasioned a greater distance between the King and Parliament than before; and it feared it will breed much disturbance.'[2]

During February that year, Princess Mary and her mother sailed to Holland, where the princess would marry the Prince of Orange and the queen could pawn the Crown Jewels to raise funds for her husband. The royal women were escorted by Prince Rupert of the Rhine, a nephew of Charles I. The king and his sons soon discovered that not everywhere welcomed them. Towns and cities had already started to take sides as to who they supported; it was an ominous sign that civil war was likely to happen in England.

Both the king and his opposition started to gather armed support; Charles within Nottingham and towards the Severn Valley, while the Parliamentarians placed official men within strategic towns and cities, as well as managing to enlist 10,000 volunteers under the leadership of the Earl of Essex. This army of volunteers was soon boosted by the Militia Ordinance and a Cambridgeshire calvary regiment, lead by Oliver Cromwell. By late summer 1642, both sides had managed to expand and multiply their armed forces and the first skirmish of the Civil Wars happened on 23 September 1642 at the Battle of Powick Bridge, near Worcester.

The first big battle of the Civil Wars was the Battle of Edgehill, which was fought a month later on 23 October 1642. Both sides gained little and both declared that they had won the battle. This indecisive outcome meant that more battles needed to be fought to declare an outright winner. Now that diplomacy and democratic process had failed, war and violence would conclusively fight it out for the governance of the nation; king versus parliament, God's anointed versus those whom the people had elected.

Battles took place throughout the rest of 1642 and 1643. The Royalists made their base in Oxford and the Parliamentarians controlled the city of London, while the divisions within the country deepened.

The Battle of Marston Moor in the summer of 1644 was the next notable encounter of the war. The city of York had been under siege from the Parliamentarians, who had joined forces with the Scots. Charles wanted to reclaim York as a royalist city and defeat both of his adversaries at the same time. However, the Parliamentarians by this time had transformed their army of volunteers from inexperienced military men into the disciplined and well-trained force of the New Model Army. In comparison, Charles' Royalist troops were untrained, undisciplined and fewer in number. On the evening of 2 July 1644, after a tense day of waiting for the expected battle to start, the Parliamentarians finally advanced at the Cavalier army at half past seven, in torrential rain. To start with, the battle went in favour of the king, until Cromwell changed the course of the battle, taking control of the Parliamentarian cavalry regiments. The battle was bloody, with heavy losses on both sides, but the Parliamentarians were victorious. As a result, the people of York surrendered to the Parliamentarians and abandoned the Royalist cause. It was a big blow for the Royalists.

The Battle of Naseby in the following summer of 1645 was another important clash between the two sides. On 14 June the Parliamentarians and Cavaliers met on the ridge at Naseby, Northamptonshire. The royal forces made the first move and attacked their enemy, but despite the fact that the Royalists were initially winning, it was Cromwell and his Parliamentarians who would change the direction of the battle by crossing into the Royalist lines. This battle marked the beginning of the end of the first Civil War.

As he was out of hope and in a desperate situation, Charles had been communicating with his former foes, the Scots. He decided after the defeat at Naseby that his best tactic was to go to his ancestral homeland of Scotland, hoping this will help win the war. Charles abandoned his royal headquarters of Oxford and headed towards his northern kingdom on 27 April 1646. He met the Scottish Presbyterian army in Newark, which escorted His Majesty to Newcastle-upon-Tyne. In Newcastle, Charles found himself held prisoner by the Scots; his northern subjects having not forgotten his attempt to reform their church. As punishment, the Scots negotiated with Westminster and the Parliamentarians and after nine months of talks, Charles was handed over to a parliamentary commission. The price of the king had been £100,000 and the pledge of more financial help in the future.

Parliament held Charles prisoner first in Northamptonshire, before moving him to Newmarket, followed by Oatlands, before finally bringing him to one of his own residences; Hampton Court. On 11 November 1647, Charles made his daring escape, arriving at the southern port of Southampton from where he travelled to the Isle of Wight. Wrongly, Charles thought that he was going to a friend in his hour of need. Unfortunately, the governor of the Isle, Colonel Robert Hammond, imprisoned the king at Carisbrooke Castle upon his arrival and then sent word to Westminster that the royal runaway had been found and was safely under lock and key.

Even though the king was incarcerated, his Cavalier supporters were able to resume fighting in his name and the Second Civil War began. The Parliamentarians were faced with insurrection and revolt on many fronts. Firstly, Charles had been communicating with the Scots again and this time they had agreed that they would invade England. The Parliamentarians and their supporters also faced insurrection and revolt in Essex, Cumberland, and Kent, as well as an uprising in the south of Wales. This did not work and all the attempts were quashed by Cromwell's powerful military machine, the New Model Army. The Second Civil War was conclusively won by the Parliamentarians in the Battle of Preston on 19 August, 1648.

Parliament attempted to keep the negotiations going with Charles, even voting on the issue in the House of Commons, the result being that 129 to 83 were in favour of negotiating and working with the defeated sovereign. Oliver Cromwell had other ideas and in December 1648, all of the members who had voted to work with the king were either arrested or wisely retired quietly from politics to their homes and families. The remaining members of parliament would go on to form the 'Rump Parliament'. This event has been described by some historians as little more than a military coup.

British politics had become a survival of the fittest and the only way in which to end this bloody civil war and move forward was for one side to deal a fatal blow to the other. That was exactly what happened. The Rump Parliament put the God-anointed king on trial and found him guilty of high treason, a crime punishable by death. Parliament had won and Charles had to die. His grandmother, Mary Queen of Scots, another God-appointed monarch and a Stuart, had also lost her head to the executioner; the precedent had been set. Charles went to his death, stepping out of the window from the Banqueting House onto a black-draped platform that had been specially erected on Whitehall. It was 30 January 1949, a chilly day, and Charles had elected to wear two shirts to keep him warm so as not to look like he was shaking from fear. That day, when Cromwell and the Puritan Republicans authorised the death of a king, they changed the course of history and politics for another half a century.

The consequences of the Civil Wars affected politics, religious views and biases, perceptions of social order and how society should or could be, as well as questioning the established political norms of an inherited monarchy, not to mention the role parliament should play in the governance of the nation.

Oliver Cromwell would also create the New Model Army during the Civil Wars, establishing a military force that was trained, equipped and disciplined. This new force would prove to be deadly effective in defeating the Royalist forces during the Civil War. Indeed, the New Model Army was so impressive that upon his restoration to the throne, Charles II would create a new, formal standing army that was as equally well-trained, disciplined and equipped. Although the New Model Army had officially been ordered to disband, two of its former regiments were incorporated into the new force to become the Royal Foot Guards and Horse Guards: the precursor to the modern British army. Although Monmouth was a strong and talented military commander, had there not been a 'modern' trained army at James II's disposal, the probability of Monmouth winning his rebellion would have been higher.

The Civil Wars had made the people weary of fighting and upon Charles II's death, there would still have been some alive who remembered the brutality of the Civil Wars and the scars that it had left, both politically and socially. These memories would have made people more wary about entering into another period of fighting: civil war turns people against their neighbours and the thought of another possible republic may also have been a deterrent which stopped people from joining Monmouth in his rebellion. It is also worth remembering that the number of people who qualified to take part in the democratic process in the late seventeenth century was very limited. Why would a farmer want to go and fight for a cause that he would have no say in?

The men who were able to engage within the political process started looking for a middle ground between an absolute monarchy and the hard-line republicanism of the Commonwealth. Men like Anthony Ashley Cooper, later created the Earl of Shaftesbury, would become more politically engaged and would not accept the concept of the Divine Right of Kings, or that the throne should automatically be inherited. This did not necessarily mean that they wanted to abolish the monarchy, but rather put restrictions upon the person who occupies the throne. The execution of the king had set a precedent; being born into the line of succession did not necessarily mean you should be given the throne or keep it, ideas that were strongly felt within Monmouth's lifetime during the Exclusion Crisis.

The cause and consequences of the Civil Wars do play a prominent and important role therefore in the understanding of the politics, society and religious views of Restoration Britain, as well as giving greater understanding to the choices that the Duke of Monmouth made and the attitudes of the people who influenced him. His rebellion can be seen as a continuation of the struggles that were fought during the Civil Wars and which would ultimately lead him on the path to lose his head upon Tower Hill.

Chapter 2

Charles II: A Life in Exile and the Birth of a Son

To put Monmouth's life into context, it is important to briefly explore what life was like for Charles II in exile while England was in the Interregnum, under the control of the Lord Protectorate, Oliver Cromwell and his victorious members of parliament.

The first aspect to note is that the initial part of Charles' time in exile was spent fighting to regain his throne. His court in exile was far from united; instead, it was divided by politics and was a viper's nest of scheming, something his court would continue to do after his restoration. Charles II's reign, therefore, started as it was to continue; full of plots, political wrestling and conflict.

Charles did attempt to look to other European counties in order to help him get back the throne. In order to succeed in this so soon after the execution of his father, Charles' best political and strategic chance of successfully re-obtaining the crown was to take the Scottish throne of his ancestral royal house, the Stuarts. There is evidence that an alliance with Charles (then still the Prince of Wales) and Scotland was being conceived as early as 1648:

> Murray's information from Scotland that their governing party there would raise an army of 20,000 men to support the Prince … to answer letters from the Committee and Assembly with gentleness; to take the Covenant if pressed to do so and to send Mr Denham to Scotland.[2]

In 1649, Charles II was conditionally declared King of Scotland on the proviso that he would agree to the terms and agreements laid down by the Covenanters. The Scots wanted their General Assembly to be recognised within England, for Presbyterianism to become the national religion of the whole country and for Charles to take the Solemn League and Covenant Oath.

Even though Charles was unhappy with these terms, he was prepared to compromise as in the circumstances, it was the best course of action available to defeat Cromwell. The negotiations proceeded and the Treaty of Breda was drawn up in the spring of 1650. By June of that year, Charles had landed in Scotland. This became the event that would spark the Third Civil War, which ultimately became a war between England and Scotland, as well as a personal and political stand off between Cromwell and Charles.

Oliver Cromwell was not going to let his Stuart foe set up court in Scotland unchallenged. Just three months after Charles had arrived in Edinburgh, the two sides clashed in the Battle of Dunbar on 3 September 1650. Charles was defeated despite having an army of 23,000; more than twice the size of Cromwell's army. The victory was a testament to the New Model Army, under the leadership of Cromwell, who had disciplined men and had invested in modern weapons. These factors and their previous experience would make up for the New Model Army's lack in numbers; on the day of the Battle of Dunbar, the New Model Army was the superior force. Charles and the Scots lost 4,000 men in the battle with an estimated additional 10,000 of his men being taken prisoner by the victors.

The defeat caused the losing side to turn in on themselves and try to apportion blame for the loss. As the Scots were arguing among themselves, Cromwell started a propaganda campaign in southern Scotland, persuading the local people that Charles' huge defeat was the will of God. With such a big defeat and so many taken prisoner, it was easy for Cromwell to use the evidence and manipulate it to his benefit. Despite Cromwell's best efforts, Charles managed to be crowned at Scone on 1 January 1651. However, Charles' reign would not last a year. On 20 July 1651, Cromwell and Charles met again on the battlefield of Inverkeithing, near Stirling. The battle was another humiliating defeat for Charles and was essentially the death knell for his support from the Scots.

Not one to give up, Charles and a group of his loyal Cavaliers travelled into the north of England in an attempt to gain a new source of support for his cause. But the north and the landed gentry were tired of fighting after long, hard years of civil conflict. At the beginning of September, Charles and his tired, defeated Cavaliers found themselves near Worcester. Cromwell had been hot on their heels after discovering that Charles had entered English territory. However, it is thought that Cromwell decided to wait before attacking Charles at Worcester in order for any battle to coincide with the date of the first anniversary of the Battle of Dunbar, 3 September. The Battle of Worcester started well for Charles. It was a dirty and bloody affair with hand-to-hand fighting during the battle, as Charles bravely found himself fighting alongside his loyal followers. As it became clear that the royal side was going to lose again, men started to defect from the Cavaliers. To his credit, Charles tried to rally his battle-weary men and stem the number of men deserting, but it was ultimately a lost cause and in the end, even he had to admit defeat and escape in order to save his own life.

What happened next was one of the most mythologised parts of Charles II's life; his escape from Worcester and his eventual return to mainland Europe. A small band of loyal Cavaliers, Buckingham among them, escaped and found themselves helped by a local Catholic family, the Pendrels. The next six weeks were spent hiding in priest holes and the folkloric 'Royal Oak' at Boscobel, with Charles even disguising himself as a wood cutter and servant during this time. He would land back in Normandy, France, on 16 October 1651, still no closer to regaining his father's throne.

Although these events happened during Monmouth's infancy, the tales of Charles' bravery and adventure would probably have been retold as part of his childhood. Charles loved his little son and it is highly probable that he would have been the person who told Monmouth these tales. Even if he had not heard these tales from his father, as a child Monmouth would have definitely heard of his father's adventures while at court. Charles was said to have been a bore on the subject and retold the stories frequently. The seventeenth century royal gossip and diarist, Samuel Pepys, received the story in all its glory from Charles and went on to publish it. Many of Charles' traits during this period of his life; his survival instincts after defeat, the rallying of supporters, the bravery in fighting and spirit of adventure, can be seen in Monmouth during his rebellion; in the skirmishes he fought, his defeat at Sedgemoor and his attempts to escape and survive. The only difference between father and son is that one survived to retell the tale many times, while the other lost his head on Tower Hill. After his grand escape from England, Charles found himself back in exile in a Europe that was in as much diplomatic and political turmoil as England.

In 1652, France was ruled by Louis XIV, who at the time was only thirteen years of age. All was not well within the French royal family. There were divisions between the King's mother and his uncle the Duke of Orleans. When Charles arrived in Paris he was not greeted by his equal, the king of France but instead by the duke.

Spain, the other Catholic superpower of seventeenth-century Europe, had turned to Cromwell's Republic in the hope that they would help them fight their long term rival, France. The French at this time were helping the Catalans, who were in dispute with the Spanish in the Catalan Revolt. The revolt had been going on since July 1651 and did not end until October 1652.

The traditional Protestant alliance with the Dutch Republic was also having its own complications. While Charles had been in Scotland and then England, the Prince of Orange had died of smallpox, the scourge of the seventeenth century. The next in line to the office of Stadtholder was William of Orange (later William III of England), who was born on 4 November 1650 at The Hague, now in the modern day territory of the Netherlands. When Charles returned to Europe, the then two-year-old William was at the centre of a row between his mother Mary, who was also Charles' sister, and the little boy's grandmother, the fierce Henrietta Maria, Dowager Queen of England. The problem was that the overbearing Catholic Henrietta Maria wanted to oversee the child's upbringing.

Upon returning to Europe, Charles initially found himself living with his mother at the Louvre, in Paris. He would move around Europe living hand-to-mouth until his restoration in 1660. Money was tight and Charles was dependent upon his mother's modest pension from the French royal family. Meals were simple and the royal household ate together. The court was lodged in local cheap accommodation. Even Clarendon, who would later be noted for his warm and luxurious rooms at Whitehall after the Restoration, lived in poverty while in exile.

For safety, Charles was forced to stay in Paris until 1654. In the summer of that year, Charles spent the time in Germany with his sister, Mary. The siblings stayed in spa towns in western Germany near Aachen and the Rhine, while also stopping in Cologne and Düsseldorf. At the end of the summer, when brother and sister went their different ways, Charles returned to Cologne for the next eighteen months. The summer had been funded by Mary, as Charles still found money tight. Indeed, by March 1656, Charles had managed to accumulate a staggering £3,200 in debt at this point in his exile.

Charles then moved on to Bruges and tried to negotiate with the Spanish, hoping that they might help him defeat Cromwell and his Commonwealth. The talks were chaired by the former Bishop of Bristol, Thomas Howell, who was able to speak Spanish. Frustratingly, nothing would come from the discussions and Charles was still further than ever before from restoring the monarchy and inheriting his father's throne.

In the late 1650s, Charles, becoming bored in Bruges, joined his younger brothers James and Henry in the Spanish army. He even took part in the Siege of Mardyke in October 1657. His relations with Spain were still cool as he had avoided conversion to Roman Catholicism. Thankfully, the situation was starting to change in England following Oliver Cromwell's death in 1658, as his son Richard struggled to maintain his father's control; Charles' time in Europe would soon be over.

Charles' exile is important to Monmouth's story as it is during this time that the politics of mainland Europe reflected the politics of Britain, both before and after the Restoration. Political plots and sub plots, were part of Monmouth's life even from his infancy and childhood in exile. His father's struggle to regain the throne may also have had an impact on Monmouth and possibly given him ideas that he too could one day claim the throne for himself, despite his status as a bastard.

Just before Charles' ill-fated attempt at trying to reclaim the Scottish throne, his first illegitimate child, James, later Duke of Monmouth and Buccleuch, Earl of Doncaster, Dalkeith, Scott of Tindale, Whitchester and Ashdale, entered the world on 9 April 1649, in the Dutch city of Rotterdam. The baby's mother was Lucy Walter, who had followed Charles' court into exile.

Lucy Walter was a mother without a husband and Charles, the baby's father, was a king without a kingdom or a crown. From his birth, Charles acknowledged James as his son, despite the fact that not everyone thought he should, including his brother James, Duke of York. These accusations stopped when Monmouth was a little boy because he was said to have been the spitting image of his father when he was a child of the same age.

Lucy Walter came from Pembrokeshire gentry and there is no evidence to suggest that her or Charles had ever met before their affair began at The Hague during July 1648. It is around this time that Monmouth was conceived. In August 1649, four months after she gave birth, Lucy Walter shared a carriage belonging to Lord Wilmore that was heading towards St Germain, Paris, with the diarist, John Evelyn. He would describe her in his diary as 'a brown, beautiful, bold but insipid creature'. This is hardly complimentary to Monmouth's mother or Charles' taste in mistresses.

While Charles headed to Scotland in 1650, the toddler was in the care of his paternal grandmother, Henrietta Maria. The reasons why baby James was in his grandmother's care are not clear. However, Lucy did not help herself if she wanted to get her child back. While Charles was in Scotland fighting at Dunbar and then later at Worcester, Lucy would go on and give birth to a second child, a daughter named Mary. Unlike her brother, Charles did not recognise this little girl as he could not have fathered the child; well substantiated rumour suggests that little Mary's father was Theobald, 2nd Viscount Taafe. It is quite possible that Lucy was in confinement for her second child, when James was under the care of Henrietta Maria.

At some point, Lucy was reunited with her son; however, it was not going to be a happy ending for her. She had by this time also taken the pseudonym of Mrs Barlow and her relationship with Charles had now soured. On 21 January 1656, the Marquis of Ormond and the Earl of Clarendon were able to persuade Lucy to accept an annual pension of £415. This was to be collected from Antwerp away from the court in order to to distance her from Charles.

Not long after this, it seems that Lucy decided to go back to England with both of her small children. Oliver Cromwell soon discovered they were back in the country and the three of them were sent to the Tower of London purely because she was known to be Charles' mistress. Lucy, James and Mary were released from the Tower on 12 July 1656. Charles' supporters in England referred to her as his wife and would serve her on their knees as if she was a royal person. Four days after their release, Lucy and her children set out for France. Upon their return, she found that she had fallen further from royal favour and as a consequence, was left with little to support herself and her children and like many before her, she was 'to abandon herself to a lewd course of life'. This, sadly, was the beginning of the end for Monmouth's mother.

One thing we can be sure of is that Lucy Walter loved her son dearly and tried, without success, to keep him with her. A letter dated 6 December from Don Alonso de Cardenas, the Spanish ambassador to London at the time, includes the following account of Lucy's struggle to keep little Monmouth with her:

> Account of the attempt made last night by Col. Slingsby to carry Mrs Barlow to one of the public prisons of the city and to separate her from her son, which she resisted with great outcries, embracing her son; the whole street was gathered together scandalized at the colonel's violence, who consented at length that the lady and her son should stay in the Earl of Castlehaven's house for the night … Mrs Barlow [is] with her son in her house, on giving her security to await knowledge of the King's will, to procure whose orders the above mentioned earl now goes.[3]

This is undoubtedly the behaviour of a woman who loves her son, but when the custody battle is between a mistress and her estranged lover, who happens to be a king, Lucy Walter realistically had no chance of winning. This is especially true when Charles is being advised in the strongest manner by Edward Hyde, the future Earl of Clarendon.

Eventually, Charles resorted to kidnap in order to get his son away from Lucy, a woman who had become little more than an embarrassment to him, his court and his reputation since his return to the continent. The following extract, dated 10 December 1657, is evidence of Charles' instructions to take the child from Lucy.

> [He] has shown the letter of 6 Dec to the King, who takes his proceeding in the business of Mrs Barlow very kindly. The King gave order to Sir Arthur Slingsby to get the child, in a quiet way if he could, out of the mother's hands with the purposes of advantage to them both, but never understood it should be attempted with that noise and scandal ... The King persists in his desire to have the child delivered into such hands as he shall appoint ... if she consent not to this, she will add to her former follies ... since neither of them will any further be cared for or owned by the King, who will take any good office done to her as an injury to him. It ought to be considered whether she should not be compelled to be good to herself or at least be restrained from ruining her innocent child by making a property of him to support herself.[4]

The inevitable happened and Lucy eventually lost her young son to Charles. Within less than a year of losing her little boy, Lucy Walter died in Paris from 'the pox'; a seventeenth century umbrella term to cover all manner of venereal and sexually contracted diseases. She breathed her last aged just twenty-seven years old. Lucy's daughter, Mary, would be adopted by the man who was rumoured to be her father, Theobald, Viscount Taaffe; a generous and unusual gesture on his part.

The relationship between Charles and Lucy has come under much scrutiny and inspired many conspiracy theories during Monmouth's own life time. The status of his parents' relationship would become important for the political arguments as to why Monmouth should be considered as an heir to the throne. Monmouth himself seems to have believed that his parents' relationship had been more than a fling and he only retracted this in a carefully worded document hours before his execution in order to ensure that his wife and children would be shown mercy and suffer no ill effects from his fall from grace. The notion that Charles had married Lucy and that there was a marriage certificate hidden in a black box was publicised by the plotter, Robert Ferguson, as propaganda to win favour for Monmouth to become Charles' heir.

There are several reasons to believe that Charles never married Lucy. Firstly, both were looking for suitors during the 1650s. Lucy was contemplating marriage to Sir Henry de Vic, an Englishman living in Brussels, and Charles was aware of this. Furthermore, Charles actively and unsuccessfully attempted to woo, 'La Grande Mademoiselle', Anne Marie Louise d'Orleans, Duchess of Montpensier. She would have been both a good political and financial match for the exiled King Charles; unfortunately, it was never to come about. Given Charles' later reputation as an unfaithful husband, La Grande Mademoiselle may just have saved herself a life of heartache by not marrying him. Neither Charles nor Lucy would have been able to pursue these avenues if they had been married to each other.

Secondly, due to her status and background, had Lucy married Charles she would not have behaved the way she did when Charles was in Scotland - behaviour that consequently resulted in the conception of a second child. She would not have done this had she been married to Charles, because to have snared a king, even a king in exile, was a massive rise in status for a girl of Lucy's social background.

Then there were always rumours of promiscuity surrounding Lucy. Would Charles, even as a king in exile, have seriously considered marrying a commoner with such a reputation, regardless of how much he thought he loved her? It would have been better for him to secure a marriage that would gain him advantages both politically and financially by marrying into another European royal family.

Lastly, if Charles had married Lucy, the exiled court circle, including the Earl of Clarendon, would not have been allowed to openly dislike and shun her as queen. Taking everything into account, it is unlikely that Charles and Lucy were ever anything more than lovers who enjoyed a brief affair during the summer before Monmouth was born.

The so-called marriage certificate that was rumoured to have been found and conveniently destroyed in the Victorian age would have been a forgery, if it ever even existed at all. This is especially true when looking at the time frame for when the supposed marriage would have likely taken place, in July 1648. Charles was on the coast with his brother James and Prince Rupert commanding the British naval fleet. He was also in the mist of negotiations with the Scots – it is therefore unlikely that he would have broken from these activities to marry a commoner, in secret, at such a time. However, a royal fumble with a willing and pretty girl is highly likely, especially given Charles' reputation as the Merry Monarch.

The way in which Charles treated his son is very telling upon the status of his relationship with the boy's mother. Although Charles acknowledged little James as his son and went on to take him from his unsuitable mother, this would have been to stop Lucy from embarrassing Charles by coming to court and using the excuse of the baby to see the king. It is unlikely to have been for the sake of the child. This is further strengthened when you consider that his son was not given the title Duke of Monmouth until after his mother's death and Charles had been restored to the throne. If the baby had been legitimate, then surely Monmouth would not have needed to be given a dukedom, he would already have been born into the title of the Prince of Wales. Charles would have been able to declare that without embarrassment after Lucy was safely dead and Charles had a new wife installed. If Monmouth had been legitimate, it would have been a lot easier for Charles to have admitted it during the Exclusion Crisis, than defend his brother the Duke of York.

It is worth mentioning that the reference to Lucy being called 'wife' is also made in letters from Charles' sister Mary, the Princess of Orange. The use of 'wife' has, for some historians, been deemed proof that Charles was married to Lucy. However, others believe that this is merely a polite way of referring to a woman who had borne Charles a child, or in reference to her status as Charles' mistress, and not their marital status.

Now in the custody of his father and at the tender age of eight-years-old, Monmouth found himself back in the care of his grandmother, the formidable Henrietta Maria, and was sent to school near Paris. His tutor was Thomas Ross Esq, a Scot, who would later become the King's Librarian. He wrote of his young pupil: 'It is a great pity so pretty a child should be in such hands as hitherto have neglected to teach him to read or tell twenty though he hath a great deal of wit and a great desire to learn.'

The result of this disjointed early education seems to have kept this 'great desire to learn' alive in Monmouth. Evidence of this can be found in his notebooks, including the notebook that was found on him when he was arrested in Ringwood, Dorset, in 1685.

CHARLES II: A LIFE IN EXILE AND THE BIRTH OF A SON

The best summary of Monmouth's childhood comes from an early twentieth century study of the duke, *On the Left of a Throne*, by Maud Nepean, which states: '[it was] known he was healthy, hearty, charming, good tempered, well mannered and handsome, qualities that he carried with him throughout his short life.'[5] Although this can be considered an overly romanticised summary of Monmouth's childhood, it is a reasonably accurate reflection of the man he grew into. When considering that he lost his mother at an early age and was then passed from his paternal grandmother to a guardian, this disruptive early life does not seem to have traumatised him or affected his personality in any drastic way.

From 1658, Monmouth took the surname of Crofts, while he lived with his guardian, Baron William Crofts of Saxham. Crofts came from a Royalist family and went into exile to serve Henrietta Maria as the captain of her guards. He would later serve Charles II as one of his Gentlemen of the Bedchamber. He has been described as a 'wild young courtier', however, he must have been highly trusted by Charles in order to make him the guardian of his first born child, a child that he had fought hard to retrieve from his mother. James Crofts, not yet a duke, would stay in Crofts' care until after the Restoration, when Lord Crofts would bring the dowager and his ward back to court in 1662. It was then that Charles, seeing his thirteen-year-old son, decided to elevate him to the dukedoms of Monmouth and Buccleuch, as well as creating him Earl of Doncaster, Dalkeith, Scott of Tindale, Whitchester and Ashdale. Monmouth's life as a courtier had begun and the people that the newly titled duke would meet, would go on to shape his fate.

Chapter 3

Restoration Politics

The restoration of the monarchy is important to Monmouth's story, as his fate is bound to the political changes within the continuation of the monarchy. There was a brief honeymoon period after Charles II became king, because after years of harsh Puritan dictatorship under Cromwell's republic, the majority of Britain was relieved to have a 'merry' monarch restored to the throne. During this period, the remaining regicides of Charles I were found and punished, although the new king's heart was not really in it. After the initial idyll, Britain found itself in an uneasy political balance of trust and co-operation between king and parliament. They tolerated each other in this uneasy truce until it finally deteriorated completely in March 1681, at the final Oxford Parliament. In many ways, the reign of Charles II was the last full sovereignty Britain would have before his brother James lost the throne and was replaced by William and Mary who ruled as a constitutional monarchy. No British monarch could use the principle of the Divine Right of Kings in the aftermath of the execution of Charles I, especially in a Protestant country. Sadly, the French did not learn from our monarchy and 144 years after the execution of Charles I, they too executed a king and his wife.

It was in these uncertain times that political factions were forced to start looking for a suitable heir to the throne who would be a manageable compromise between monarchy and parliament. When it became apparent that there would be no legitimate issue from Charles II's wife, Queen Catherine of Braganza, Monmouth, although illegitimate, fitted the popular and politically correct requirement of being a Protestant. This in turn made him very appealing to the anti-Catholic fledgling Whig party, who felt that they could 'manage' him as a monarch, rather than James II.

Charles set sail for England from the Dutch coast on 23 May 1660. England, Ireland and Scotland were entering a new chapter in their joint histories, as the United Kingdoms of Great Britain, and Charles was coming home to lands that had suffered at the hands of Cromwell. He made a triumphant entry into London on 29 May 1660, which also happened to be his thirtieth birthday. The streets were lined with cheering crowds welcoming their dashing and handsome monarch back. The diarist, John Evelyn, a contemporary of Samuel Pepys, described what he saw when Charles re-entered London:

> This day, his Majesty, Charles the second came to London, after a sad and long exile and calamitous suffering both of the king and church, being seventeen years. This was also his birth-day, and with a triumph of above 20,000 horse and foot, brandishing their swords and shouting with inexpressible joy; the ways strewed with flowers, the bells ringing, the streets hung with tapestry. Fountains running with wine; the mayor, alderman, and all the companies in their liveries chains of gold and banners; lords and nobles, clad in cloth of silver, gold and velvet; the windows and balconies all set with ladies, trumpets, music and myriads of people flocking, even so far as from Rochester so as they were seven hours in passing the city, even from two in the afternoon til nine at night.[6]

Evelyn continued his eyewitness account saying:

> I stood in the strand and beheld it and blessed God. And all this was done without one drop of blood shed, and by that very army which rebelled against him: but it was the Lords doing, for such a restoration was never mentioned in any history, ancient or modern since the return of the Jews from their Babylonish captivity; nor so joyful a day and so bright ever seen in this nation, this happening when to expect or effect it was past all human policy.[7]

To understand the politics that affected the events in Monmouth's life, it is important to have a basic comprehension of the political history of the early Restoration and the differences between the political factions and key players. As monarchy and republicanism are at the extreme polar opposites on the political and social spectrum, it is always going to mean that whatever compromise is reached, both sides will be displeased to an extent. Due to the nature of British republicanism at the time, there was the added complication of incorporated Puritanism that sparked extreme views backed up by religious belief.

At this time, Britain was still scarred from the traumatic years of civil unrest from a nation at war with itself. If that had not damaged the nation enough, this was then followed by a decade of repressive republicanism. The return of Charles and his merry court must have been a welcome relief.

Had the self-styled Lord Protector, Oliver Cromwell, lived another ten years, republicanism may well have continued in Britain. Thankfully, his son Richard failed to hold the nation as his father had done. Happily, General George Monck could see more clearly than many what was happening to England, and he decided that restoring Charles II to the throne was the best solution. At the beginning of the Civil Wars, Monck had been on the Royalist side. However, Charles decided to oust him from his post of Governor of Dublin. Not unsurprisingly, a resentful Monck changed sides and fought with Cromwell in the Battle of Dunbar (1650). During the republican rule, Monck received correspondence from an exiled Charles II. Unlike Cromwell, Monck seems not to have been a republican to the core, although this was probably pragmatism and to aid political survival.

After three unsuccessful parliaments had been called in 1659, Britain had become unstable and Monck decided to leave Scotland and restore peace through the restoration of the Stuart monarchy. Once he arrived in London in February 1660, Monck became the catalyst that started the dissolution of the failed Long Parliament, which was finally completed on 16 March 1660. Monck played a key role in the creation of the Convention Parliament which would decide to invite Charles II back to England. The final step to restoration, in which Monck was instrumental, was to finalise the terms of the Treaty of Breda, setting out the conditions for Charles' return.

The early parliamentary sessions until the beginning of 1679 have become known as the Cavalier Parliament and over the eighteen and a half years it held eighteen sessions. In some ways, the Cavalier Parliament worked along similar lines to the one we are familiar with today. There were two houses, the Commons that were elected and the Lords, made up of hereditary peers of the realm as well as Church of England Bishops. The biggest difference between Charles' Cavalier Parliament and the current House of Commons is that there were no formalised or official political parties, leaders or ministers running the country. Issues were debated by elected representatives and subsequently voted on due to an individual's views, morals or how it would affect their lives. The members of both the Houses of Commons and Lords roughly separated into two factions of ideas; the Court faction and the Country faction. Membership of these groups were transitory and dependent upon policy or issue being debated within the chambers.

It is also important to note that one of the keys to understanding seventeenth-century politics, as well as the story of Monmouth, is the role that religious belief played in politics. This in turn meant that Christian denominations turned against each other and in a Protestant nation there was a true fear of Catholicism when it was practiced by those in politics and by those close to the monarchy. This was a legacy of the reformation triggered by Henry VIII in the sixteenth century, as well as the wider European reformation and subsequent counter-reformation that ended up dividing Europe. This division within the European mainland created both allies and enemies as well as associating Catholicism with absolutism and tyranny. In comparison, Protestantism represented ideas of limited democracy and freedom of thought.

There was a fluidity to the affiliation of the political factions of the mid-seventeenth century after the Restoration. However, broadly speaking, MPs who were part of the Country faction were pro-Protestant, both domestically and internationally, and protective of the rights of parliament and democracy; they would later become concerned about the monarch's encroachment of these political, social and parliamentary rights. Among the leading figures of this movement were Lord Cavendish, William Lord Russell and after 1674, Lord Shaftesbury and the Duke of Buckingham.

The Court faction is harder to define. Firstly, they were not united in faith, having varied religious backgrounds and different ideas on foreign policy. The one political concept that they all held firm and believed in was the powers and rights of the monarch. Many of the Country circle had fathers who had fought for the Cavaliers in the Civil Wars and some had been in exile with Charles during the frustrating period of Cromwell's Interregnum. Included within the Court faction was a cabal who formed a Restoration Privy Council and would become the closest advisers to King Charles. They were: Thomas Clifford, 1st Baron Clifford of Chudleigh; Henry Bennet, 1st Earl of Arlington; George Villiers, 2nd Duke of Buckingham; Antony Ashley Cooper, 1st Baron Ashley and John Maitland, 1st Duke of Lauderdale.

There were other men who were part of this circle, however, these five were the core and primary members of this group. These men, like Charles, were generally pro-French in terms of foreign policy, as well as being more tolerant of other religious denominations such as Catholics and deserter denominations of Christianity such as the Quakers and Puritans. This is why the Court faction is harder to define in ideology. For example, the Earl of Clarendon, Edward Hyde, was part of this group, but he was most certainly not tolerant of other religious denominations or pro-French. He was, however, a monarchist to the core of his political being.

Edward Hyde, later the Earl of Clarendon, would rise to be a political big wig within the Restoration court and be a primary adviser to King Charles II. He would also become the maternal grandfather to two English queens; Mary II, who reigned with her husband, William of Orange, and tragic Queen Anne. However, his beginnings were humble. Hyde started his political career as MP for Wootton Bassett in April 1640 and was an MP in the short parliament. Seven months later, when parliament reconvened in the November of the same year, Hyde became MP for Saltash.

Despite the fact that he rose to be one of the most trusted advisers to both Charles I and II, Hyde started his political career as a temperate critic of King Charles I. The one political view that Hyde always defended was that the monarchy should have unrestricted powers, due to his belief in the Divine Right of Kings. Through his championing of this idea of the royal prerogative, Hyde would end up supporting the man whom he had intentionally criticised, Charles I.

The final turning point in Hyde's early political career happened when parliament presented the Grand Remonstrance to Charles I in December 1641. From this point, Edward Hyde rose swiftly up the political ladder, and was appointed Chancellor of the Exchequer in February 1643. Among the royal circle, Hyde had a reputation for having conservative views in all areas of politics. This conservative view had been his standpoint during the exile of Charles II. However, what made him a sensible and good adviser in times of exile would prove boring and pompous in the opulent and frivolous court of the early years of the Restoration government.

After the execution of the king, Hyde joined Charles II in exile on mainland Europe. He would become Charles' chief adviser and he was rewarded for his dedication in 1658, when he was officially appointed Lord Chancellor. It was Hyde who advised Charles, in the strongest possible terms, that he should rid himself of his fallen mistress; Lucy Walter.

It was not just Monmouth's mother that Clarendon was unfavourable towards. He was less than charmed by a young James Crofts, the future Duke of Monmouth, arguing that he was 'too young and inexperienced to have a dukedom conferred on him'. Charles would ignore Hyde's advice and on St Valentine's day, 1663, James Crofts received his dukedom.

Edward Hyde is important to Monmouth's life story in two ways. Firstly, he was a key witness to the early Restoration court, thus providing us with many insights into the people of the court, as well as politics and the key events of the period. Secondly, Clarendon was a key player in the negotiations that brought about the marriage of Charles II to Catherine of Braganza. When it became apparent that Charles' wife, Queen Catherine, was unlikely to give him the much-needed heir, Hyde's enemies said that he had known, at the time of their marriage, that Catherine was unable to have children. This was twisted further when others said he used this knowledge to ensure that his grandchildren, via James Duke of York and his daughter Anne, would eventually inherit the throne. In the seventeenth century it is very unlikely that Clarendon could possibly have known in advance that Catherine would have had fertility problems. To blame Clarendon for this is not only over simplistic, but actually implausible in a time when medical science, especially gynaecology and obstetrics, were in their infancy. At the time, female health issues and pregnancy were overseen by local wise women, who relied upon old wives' tales and their experience on such matters. Fate was unkind to Edward Hyde, a man who had only ever loyally served the king and his father before him.

Politics in the seventeenth century was notoriously fickle and in the libertine court of Charles II, the conservative advice of the Earl of Clarendon was never going to be respected or appreciated. As a consequence, Hyde would attract powerful enemies within the Restoration court and its parliament. He fell from grace after a catalogue of problems and rumours blaming him as the cause of these issues. This included the ridiculous accusation that he knew Queen Catherine was barren and that he was to blame for the Fire of London. The final nail in his political coffin was the unpopular religious and political codes that bore his name. In order to find a way to get rid of him, the Earl became the convenient scapegoat to blame for the Anglo-Dutch wars and the losses suffered. He was eventually impeached in 1667 and forced into retirement. He went to Rouen, France, where he died alone and gouty seven years later, in December 1674. His son would bring his mortal remains home for burial at Westminster Abbey. Edward Hyde, Earl of Clarendon did not therefore live to see the downfall of the Duke of Monmouth, whom he felt was 'too young and inexperienced', nor to see the triumph of his granddaughters take the throne of Great Britain.

Unlike his contemporaries, Shaftesbury or Clarendon, George Savile, Earl of Halifax, was somewhat of a political free spirit. During his political career, Halifax did not commit to one faction or idea in politics. He joined the

Restoration court in 1660 and seems to have slipped in and out of Whitehall sporadically. However, he did have one passionate belief that was evident throughout his politics; his anti-Catholic stance. This meant that he had an intense dislike of the king's brother, the Catholic James, Duke of York. It is therefore quite surprising that during the Exclusion Crisis, Halifax helped Charles to defeat the Lords from passing the Exclusion Bill, especially in that he was the nephew of leading Exclusionist, Anthony Ashley Cooper, Lord Shaftesbury.

Despite criticising his uncle for his patronage of the Duke of Monmouth in 1680, Halifax would also do likewise and support the Duke in 1684. There is, however, no evidence that this was a long term association with Monmouth or that Halifax was in anyway involved in the rebellion of 1685. Indeed, if he had been, James II would have taken this opportunity to be rid of one of his most ardent opponents. Halifax would go on to become one of the leading facilitators of the Glorious Revolution in 1688, which would see his nemesis James deposed and William and Mary established as the new constitutional monarchs of Great Britain.

Leading early radical Whig politician and prominent Exclusionist MP, Anthony Ashley Cooper, 1st Earl of Shaftesbury, played a key role within the Exclusion Crisis. He was born in 1621, but had found himself orphaned by the tender age of eight with a fortune and baronetcy. This sad beginning did not stop Cooper. He would go on to attend Exeter College, Oxford, though he left minus a degree, instead following a law career at Lincoln's Inn, London. This career opening was due to his first father-in-law, the 1st Baron Coventry. He married Margaret Coventry in 1639 and through this marriage, Cooper was able to enter politics at the young age of nineteen.

He won his first parliamentary seat in the Short Parliament during the spring of 1640, becoming the Member of Parliament for the constituency of Tewkesbury & Gloucestershire. In the autumn of the same year, he was not asked to stand again for the same constituency as part of the Long Parliament elections. This was due in part to the fact that his father-in-law had fallen out of favour with other prominent Royalists. Cooper tried to be re-elected to the Long Parliament through a by-election for Downton in Wiltshire, but despite winning the required number of votes he was blocked from entering the Commons by Denzil Holles. Holles was a prominent and outspoken MP who despite disliking Charles I, was never a hardline Republican. In many ways, Cooper and Holles shared similar political aims and it was Cooper's close links to the Royal household that Holles felt might make him more sympathetic towards Charles' cause. It is worth remembering that 'democratically elected' in the seventeenth and eighteenth centuries was not quite how we understand the term in the twenty-first century; few (and naturally only men) had the right to vote. MPs were only selected from the ruling classes, reflecting only a tiny minority of the country's population. Rivals, family and the whim of the monarch were all factors that had as much influence in the results of an election as the popular vote. It was certainly a matter of not what, but who you knew and how you could influence them.

For the first two years of the Civil Wars, Cooper was loyal to the Royalists and Charles I. Eventually his political split from the Royalists was due to a disagreement with Prince Maurice of the Palatinate, the elder brother of Prince Rupert of the Rhine. The Prince allowed his men to rampage and sack the southern towns of Dorchester and Weymouth, after Cooper had given his word to the two towns that they would be spared from such greedy and disrespectful acts of war. It was Prince Maurice who went on to hold a grudge after an altercation between himself and Cooper. The Prince, in a petty act of revenge, attempted to block Cooper's promotion to the position of the Governor of Weymouth and Portland, claiming that he disapproved of Cooper's appointment on the grounds of his youth and lack of political and life experience. Cooper appealed to his future rival, Edward Hyde, who was at this time the Chancellor of the Exchequer. Hyde helped Cooper, enabling him to take the position of Governor under the proviso that he resign after a suitable and dignified period of holding the position, in order to appease the pompous Prince and his unwarranted concerns.

In the first part of 1644, Cooper changed his allegiance in the Civil Wars. He resigned all his posts under Charles I, feeling that the king was under the influence of too many Catholics at court. Cooper said that his conscience therefore dictated that it was just and right to join the Parliamentarian cause so he could help uphold the Protestant faith in England. These ideals about upholding the Anglican communion for the nation would be at the centre of Cooper's future politics during the Restoration, and was at the crux of the Exclusion Crisis.

The next significant chapter in Cooper's career began in 1652, when he was appointed to the Hale Committee during the Rump Parliament. Although none of the proposals made by the committee were actioned, the fact that Cooper, who was a political turncoat, had been asked to be part of a Republican parliamentary committee, shows his skill at political survival. This approval was reiterated in 1653 when Cromwell nominated him to stand in the election as one of the MPs for the county of Wiltshire. This parliamentary session was known as Barebones Parliament or Little

Parliament and during it, Cooper aligned himself with the moderate politicians, a good survival strategy during the early period of Cromwell's Republic. The session's unusual name came from the fact that it drastically cut the number of MPs in order to avoid the return of those who were pro-Monarchist. Technically, it was an appointed assembly rather than an elected government, and was made up of 129 men representing England, 5 for Scotland and 6 for Ireland (although these representatives were all English anyway). The appointment of these men also reduced the number of candidates from the ruling classes. The most important function of the Barebones Parliament was that it prepared the way for the induction of the Protectorate government, with Cromwell as the Lord Protectorate of England, Scotland and Ireland.

In the next election, held in 1654 under the first Protectorate Parliament, Cooper was elected for Tewksbury, but his political alliance with Cromwell would soon deteriorate. By early 1655, Cooper was concerned that Cromwell was ruling through the fear and force of the New Model Army, i.e. in a military dictatorship, rather than through his parliament. True to his political nature, Cooper preferred to change matters legally rather than by force. Cooper's decision to stand up to Cromwell would affect his political career until the Restoration.

In the second Protectorate Parliament in autumn 1656, Cooper and ninety-nine other former politicians from the previous parliament were excluded from forming part of the new government. Cooper was not going to agree to this autocratic and unlawful action without protest. Along with sixty-five other excluded former members of Parliament, he signed a petition objecting to this undemocratic proceeding. Eventually, he was allowed back to take part in the government in early 1658, during what would be Cromwell's last Parliament.

After Cromwell's death in late 1658, his son Richard assumed his father's role as Lord Protector. Richard, however was not his father's son and was not only a weak leader but also politically uncharismatic. During the third Protectorate Parliament, Cooper, being the astute political animal that he was, felt the shift in political power and spoke out in the Commons against the bill that sanctioned Richard Cromwell as his father's replacement. Cooper wanted Richard to have less power and control over the New Model Army and within parliament. He was a politician ahead of his time.

Things finally broke down in parliament in autumn 1659 when the New Model Army dissolved the Rump Parliament. This did not stop Cooper from being politically active as he was part of a group of men, including

Henry Nevill and Sir Arthur Haselrig, who continued to meet regularly after the dissolution. They would discuss political ideas and how they saw the political future of Great Britain, as well as to try and work out how best to resolve the political quagmire England found herself in. It was this group of men that would eventually approach Sir George Monck, taking the first steps towards the Restoration of Monarchy.

On Boxing Day 1659, the Rump Parliament reassembled with Monck's aid. Cooper took a leading role in advising Monck on how to deal with the Rump Parliament during the early part of 1660. Once again, Monck, as well as Cooper, demonstrated their political survival skills by being drawn towards the possibility that restoring the monarchy would be the solution to the country's problems. Through looking at how Cooper voted during this time we can see that he went from favouring a conditional restoration to an unconditional restoration. He came around to the idea of restoration so much that he was part of the company who went to The Hague to meet Charles and helped draw up the declaration of Breda. Ever the political animal, Cooper would ensure that he received an official pardon for his political association with Cromwell's Commonwealth during the negotiations.

Cooper's luck continued into the summer of 1660 after Charles II was finally restored to the British throne. The new regime had so much trust in him as an ally and politician, that he took a prominent role in the trial and conviction of the regicides who had signed the death warrant of Charles I, as part of the Indemnity and Oblivion Act of 1660. Cooper was therefore partly responsible for the convicting of traitors by ensuring that they were tried and given traitors' deaths. Some of the men whom Cooper helped to convict had worked with him during the Cromwellian republic. Once again, Cooper showed that he was able and willing to work with the government and make difficult choices for his political and physical survival.

The issue of Cooper's dislike of the encroachment of Catholicism towards the British throne would resurface in Restoration politics as early as 1661. Cooper objected to Charles' choice of bride, Catherine of Braganza, primarily because she was Catholic and secondly due to the fact that she was Portuguese, who at the time, were allied with France against Spain. It was over this issue that Cooper and Edward Hyde, Earl of Clarendon (from whom he had previously sought help) now became political rivals, which would turn into a deep-set rivalry that would last until Clarendon's downfall six years later.

Having established his pro-Protestant politics, the next notable episode in Cooper's career is when he and Monmouth first met in 1665. They were introduced by none other than Charles II himself, during a visit to Cooper's estate in Wimborne, St Giles. The results of this fateful meeting would climax twenty years later on Tower Hill.

At the start of the 1670s Cooper fell out of favour with Charles, the reason being that he was pushing the king to divorce Queen Catherine, as she was proving unable to conceive the much-needed male Stuart heir. It had become apparent that Charles was not the problem within the marriage, as he had fathered several illegitimate children, including Monmouth. The lack of any issue, particularly male children, was evidently not down to the king's biology. The reason Cooper raised this provocative and risky subject with Charles was because the Duke of York, the current heir to the throne, had recently converted to Catholicism and married again after the death of his first wife, Anne Hyde. York's new bride was the Catholic Mary of Modena. As a result, Cooper feared that if the Duke of York inherited the throne and subsequently produced male issue, then Anglican Protestantism would no longer be the national faith.

A consequence of Cooper pushing his opinion to the king on this personal matter was that he lost his position as Lord Chancellor. Cooper was also unaware that the Secret Treaty of Dover with France had been signed, and that Charles was now taking money from his Catholic cousin Louis XIV of France, in exchange for finding a way to reconvert Britain to the church in Rome. The Duke of York's conversion would have helped smooth things over with Louis. The ground was now prepared for the policy of Exclusion to germinate with the possible influence of Cooper's friend and personal doctor, John Locke.

Although Cooper had displeased the king over his opinions relating to Queen Catherine, in terms of her inability to have children and suitability to remain queen, Charles still rewarded him for his political support for the Royal Declaration of Indulgence. This declaration was Charles' attempt to bring about the end of any penal laws that repressed religious liberty to non-Anglicans, such as Catholics and nonconformists, including Quakers. The penal laws often stopped men from pursuing political office due to their personal belief. In the list of honours announced in April 1672, Anthony Ashley Cooper was honoured with the title Earl of Shaftesbury; which is how he is most commonly known and remembered by history.

The next important event that links Shaftesbury to Monmouth's story happens in the following spring, when the Test Act became law. The law made it a legal requirement that all those in political or court offices must take the Protestant Anglican communion and renounce the act of Transubstantiation. This central doctrine of the Catholic faith is the belief that the bread and wine used in Holy Communion turn into the literal body and blood of Jesus Christ, rather than just symbolising them. Shaftesbury and Monmouth fulfilled their requirement to meet with the Test Act together in the London church of St Clement Danes, with John Locke as their witness. The king's brother, the Duke of York, refused to comply with the Test Act conditions and spurned receiving the Anglican communion, despite being in the office of Lord High Admiral of the Royal Navy. This would once again rouse Shaftesbury to confront Charles to divorce Catherine and seek to marry a Protestant wife in order to father Protestant heirs. Politically, Shaftesbury had tried to ensure the Protestant line of succession and failed. The great political survivor would once more change political alliances and move away from the Restoration court faction and towards the Country political faction, which would later evolve into the Whig party.

Shaftesbury put his cards on the table during the new parliamentary session that started in January 1674, with his anti-Catholic stance. The beginning of the Whig party can be traced to this time, when like-minded politicians, who were also opposed to a Catholic succession, started to meet frequently. As well as Shaftesbury, other leading Whigs included the Earl of Carlisle, the Earl of Salisbury, the Duke of Buckingham, Viscount of Halifax and Baron Holles. They would meet and discuss the issues of succession at Holles' home. During these meetings, alternative policies are highly likely to have been discussed, including the exclusion of the Duke of York from the throne and who they favoured to replace him; Monmouth, or William of Orange and York's eldest daughter, Mary.

Both Salisbury and Shaftesbury would attack leading Catholics, especially the Duke of York, by trying to introduce a law that would ensure that York's subsequent children from his second wife should be raised in the traditional Anglican church, or be excluded from inheriting the British throne. This did not come into being and the anti-Catholic faction were starting to become politically frustrated. They became so frustrated that they almost accused the Duke of York of High Treason on the grounds that his religion was harmful to the throne and kingdom. Charles heard of these plans being plotted by Shaftesbury and his cronies, and decided to take matters into his own hands by ending the parliamentary session and ensuring that the Duke of York was not accused of High Treason. The consequences of his involvement with these accusations cost Shaftesbury his place on the

Privy Council, as well as the good will of the king, and he was exiled from London. This was a high personal cost for Shaftesbury, who was trying to change the law to protect the nation's faith.

Politically, Shaftesbury continued in this vein during the next parliamentary session of late 1675. He spoke out in the House of Lords claiming that the Bishops and Thomas Osborne, 1st Duke of Leeds and Earl of Danby, were attempting to reduce the power of the House of Lords. The reasoning for this was to strengthen the political power of the Anglican elected MPs and thus reduce the voice and influence of any Catholic hereditary Lords, which in turn mirrored Danby's own political agenda. At the crux of his argument, Shaftesbury stated that monarchs ruled either through the nobility of the country or through an army. By reducing the power of the House of Lords, Shaftesbury argued that this was going against the grain of Magna Carta of 1215, which had forced the reduction of power from the monarchy and given more influence to the ruling classes.

Men such as Danby belonged to what is known as the Court faction, which would eventually evolve into the Tory Party, and was primarily made up of Royalists from the Civil Wars and Commonwealth years. Many of the faction were either Catholic or Anglican, rather than reformist Protestant, and originated from within the gentry. The thought of excluding James, Duke of York from the throne due to his Catholic faith would have been irreconcilable to their politics, especially when the suggested alternative to the lawful heir was the king's illegitimate son. The Court faction was less open to a more 'democratic' form of government, holding firm with the idea of the Divine Right of Kings and that a Monarch should rule and be head of the government, and not rule alongside a government. Compared to the Country faction, who were widely appealing to the populace at large, the Court faction were exactly as their name suggests; they were made up of a small, elitist minority close to the monarch. They were traditionalists and in all fairness more worried about maintaining their favour with Charles rather than the good of the nation.

In terms of Monmouth's story, the Earl of Shaftesbury is important because he had lived through times of civil unrest, both socially and politically. The strong political beliefs he had regarding the inheritance of the throne and the importance of maintaining the Anglican faith through the role of the monarch, can be traced back through his early political career. It is easy to see why he may have favoured Monmouth over the Duke of York as the future heir. It is worth remembering, when looking at his motives for working with and promoting Monmouth, that if Shaftesbury had not died, he probably would have abandoned him when he became less politically useful. This begs the question of how much of a friend Shaftesbury really was to the duke? It is possible that Shaftesbury would have championed William and Mary at the death of Charles II, rather than Monmouth and his risky rebellion, although this is purely speculation.

The philosopher John Locke is worth mentioning briefly, because although he was not directly involved with the Duke of Monmouth and his fate, he was associated with Shaftesbury, and modern historians now believe that his political writings on government and monarchy are about Exclusion, rather than the Glorious Revolution, as previously thought.

Six years after the Restoration, Locke met Shaftesbury in Oxford while he was looking for medical help with a particularly nasty kidney infection. The pair got along so well that Locke became part of Shaftesbury's household at Exeter House in the capacity of his personal doctor. During this time, Locke performed a lifesaving operation to remove a cyst from Shaftesbury's kidney. During the seventeenth century, going under a surgeon's knife was a great gamble and Shaftesbury would later say that Locke saved his life.

Locke became politically active at the same time that Shaftesbury became Lord Chancellor in 1672. However, when Shaftesbury fell out of favour with Charles in 1673, Locke headed to Europe until Shaftesbury's political star rose again. In 1679, Locke was back in London and started to work on his *Treatise of Government* that considered the role of monarchy and was used as an argument against absolutism. It is highly probable that Shaftesbury and Locke would have debated and discussed such issues, and the latter may have helped Shaftesbury form his ideas and policies about Exclusion.

Although there is no evidence to prove that Locke was involved in the Rye House Plot in 1683, he still fled the country with Shaftesbury, probably as part of Shaftesbury's household, rather than for fear of being accused of involvement. After Shaftesbury's death, he would stay in the Netherlands until 1688 and was therefore not in England during the end of Charles II's reign, or for Monmouth's rebellion. However, both Locke and Monmouth were in exile within the same region and as former associates of Shaftesbury, it is highly likely that the Duke of Monmouth and Locke may have met in mutual company, although there is no direct evidence to suggest that Locke influenced Monmouth in any way during this time, or in the run up to his rebellion.

It was during the period that has become known as the Exclusion Parliaments between 1679 and 1681 that the first political parties, as we would recognise them, started to emerge in the form of the Whigs and the Tories. These infant parties would have different ideological views on state politics and religion. As Tim Harris, in his *Politics Under the Later Stuarts* puts it:

> The crisis over the succession did produce a polarisation between two fairly well identified sides, both of which had distinct political ideologies and processed a rudimentary degree of organisation, however the party battle was about much more than exclusion; it involved a whole range of issues which had been sources of political tension since the Restoration ... constitutionally both sides embraced a broad spectrum of positions.[8]

It was also during this time that MPs such as Shaftesbury started seeing Monmouth as a potentially viable option to be the heir to the throne, instead of the Duke of York. Ultimately, it was because men like Shaftesbury failed within the political arena to achieve their goals that plots emerged to achieve the same objectives; unfortunately, Monmouth would become the figurehead and focus of these men's politically motivated and ambitious schemes. The ending of parliament in 1681 was the beginning of a period of serious plotting involving Monmouth.

The first of the Exclusion parliaments lasted five months, from 6 March until 12 July 1679. The topic of Exclusion entered parliament because the Duke of York had been discovered to have been corresponding with both Rome and Louis XIV of France. The Commons felt this was encouraging conspiracies against both the king and Protestantism.

Ever the diplomat, Charles tried to smooth this over by suggesting that any Catholic successors should have less freedoms as monarch than he had as a Protestant monarch, but this was never going to pacify the hardline Exclusionists, led by Shaftesbury. The first reading of the Exclusion Bill took place on 15 May 1679, with the second on 21 May. When the House voted, the bill was passed by 207 votes to 127. Parliament had displeased Charles by voting in favour of excluding his brother, and so to avoid the bill going any further, Charles exercised his royal prerogative and dissolved parliament on 12 July. This was not a democratic move and would only increase fears that Charles was turning into his autocratic father.

The second Exclusion Parliament was called in October 1679. The reason why Charles recalled parliament was because he had failed to secure further funds from the French and he needed more money. But Parliament was not going to let the matter of Exclusion drop. They knew that they held the upper hand and why Charles had recalled them. In the intervening three months between the two Exclusion parliaments, Shaftesbury had been busy gaining additional support for the policy of Exclusion. As a result of this recruiting to his cause, Shaftesbury found himself further out of favour with Charles, who in turn dismissed him from the Privy Council. It was due to the Exclusion agenda in parliament that Charles would go on and prorogue parliament six more times during 1680; on 26 January, 15 April, 17 May, 1 July, and 23 August, until finally calling it to session on 21 October 1680. Despite Charles' efforts to trying and quieten Shaftesbury, there was still great support for the Exclusionists in both the upper and lower chambers of Parliament. The Exclusion Bill passed three readings in the Commons and made it to the Lords.

This time Charles attended the debates in the House of Lords and with help from George Savile, Earl of Halifax, the king got his way when Halifax was able to persuade the undecided Lords to vote, as Charles wanted, against Exclusion. The bill failed sixty-three to thirty. When the Lords failed to pass the bill, they tried to tempt Charles with money by offering him £600,000 in exchange for agreeing to Exclusion. Charles' answer was to once again prorogue Parliament.

The third and final Exclusion Parliament was also the last parliament of Charles reign, and was called by the king in March 1681. However, Charles wanted a firm hold on this Parliament and so exercised his power as monarch. It was in fact the last time a British monarch would wield such powers within a parliamentary setting. His first act was to move parliament from the Exclusionist stronghold of London to the traditionally Royalist city of Oxford. The theory behind this was that by moving the pro-Exclusion MPs from their core supporters and comfortable surroundings, their zeal for the policy of Exclusion would diminish. Like all radicals, the Exclusionists were not to be weakened by a mere change of parliamentary location.

Charles was able to dissolve this last parliament because he had finalised the Secret Treaty of Dover with the French, so that he was no longer dependent upon his government for money. The terms of the treaty granted Charles a down payment of £40,000 and then an annual pension of £115,000 for the next three years, on the proviso that he did not recall parliament during this period.

In a last ditch attempt to pacify the Exclusion faction of his government, Charles suggested that when he died and James inherited the throne, William and Mary should rule as regents and that James be king in name alone, with none of the powers of the monarchy that he himself exercised. This suggestion was unsurprisingly rejected by parliament and after just a week in session, the last parliament of Charles II's reign was dissolved.

Chapter 4

The Religious Legacy of the English Reformation within the Restoration Court

Much of the social anxiety and deep seated fear and suspicion that was present in the Protestant establishment within Charles' Restoration court, was a hangover from the previous century's reformation and the resulting Counter-Reformation that continued into the seventeenth century and beyond. Europe was on the cusp of leaving a religious mindset of tradition and ritual, and struggling with the conception of the enlightenment. The religious questioning that started with the Reformation would affect both European and domestic politics for the rest of the seventeenth century.

Within England and Scotland, which were not yet legally bound as the United Kingdom of Great Britain, these suspicions and fears of the Church of Rome had been heightened by the Commonwealth under the tyrannical incumbency of Oliver Cromwell and his Puritan Parliamentarians. However, the religious climate within Europe at the time of the Restoration also helps to explain the domestic climate of anti-Catholicism, why the Exclusion Crisis emerged, and why the Duke of Monmouth became the Exclusionists' Protestant poster boy and subsequently a failed rebel for the Protestant cause.

Mainland Europe at the time of the Restoration was in the grips of the Counter-Reformation, headed by the dominant and powerful Catholic nations of Europe; France, Spain and Italy. The Counter-Reformation had pushed Protestantism north to Scandinavia, northern German provinces, and into the Dutch Republic. England and Scotland were also predominantly Protestant, but due to their geographical separation from the European mainland, were less likely to be a Protestant problem to the Catholic powers. England, and in particular the area of Spitalfields in East London, had become a Protestant refuge for French Protestants (Huguenots). This had slowly started to happen after Henry IV had signed the Edict of Nantes in 1598. The agreement itself was supposed to provide a general level of tolerance towards the Huguenots, but many still found themselves feeling less than welcome in France, and had therefore begun to seek refuge in more tolerant countries. This proved to be a wise move, especially when Louis XIV revoked the edict in 1685.

The heads of state at the forefront of the Counter-Reformation sweeping through Europe were the French monarch, King Louis XIV, also known as the Sun King and Spanish Habsburg Monarch, Charles II. Both these kings were Catholic and absolute monarchs. After the brief period of republicanism that had failed after the death of Cromwell, the Restoration, although welcomed by many, was still viewed by some with suspicion, primarily from Protestants who feared that a restored monarchy would follow the example of the French and Spanish reigns. Although the restored Charles II was of the Protestant faith, was the head of the Anglican Church of England and had agreed to work with his Parliament (unlike his French cousin Louis), the fact that Charles would go on to marry a Portuguese Catholic Infanta would only increase these fears of absolutism further among those political classes and former parliamentarians of England.

Naively, Charles hoped to create a society that allowed all Christian denominations to practice their religion freely and as their conscience dictated. However, this Utopian idea of religious tolerance was not to happen during his reign. These ideas of toleration would also fuel and tighten the king's adversaries' suspicions about whether Charles was in fact secretly Catholic. This in turn ignited the arguments of the Exclusionists, which subsequently drew them to look towards the Protestant Duke of Monmouth as an heir, despite his illegitimate status.

Closer to home, there was good cause for the English collective psyche to be wary of a Catholic monarchy and reign. Firstly, there was the history of Catholic conspiracies and intrigues that had taken place on English soil. Among these stratagems were the plots involving Mary Queen of Scots, which had aimed to displace the Protestant Queen Elizabeth I for the Catholic Mary. The most famous of these plots are the Throckmorton Plot of 1583 and the Babington Plot of 1586, which in turn would lead to Mary's arrest, conviction and execution. Closer in time and still possibly even within living memory for some of Charles' older subjects, was the Gunpowder Plot, in which Catholic extremists intended to blow up the British (Protestant) monarchy and establishment at the state opening of parliament in 1605.

Then there was the history of the last Catholic monarch to grace the British throne, Mary Tudor, who is better known as 'Bloody Mary', the eldest daughter of Henry VIII. She gained her nickname for the hundreds of Protestants she persecuted and burnt at the stake for their religious beliefs. She may only have had four years on the throne, but the damage that she caused to her Protestant subjects lived long in the Protestant nation's collective memories. These memories of Protestant martyrs were kept alive through the publication of John Foxe's *Book of Martyrs*, detailing the deaths of those who died under Queen Mary's English Counter-Reformation. No wonder the thought of a possible new Catholic monarch, in the form of James, Duke of York brought fear to the Protestant populace of England.

Closer to home was Catholic Ireland, then a dominion of the British crown, which had been a Catholic thorn in England's side both before and during the Commonwealth, the most recent rebellion there taking place in 1641. Under Cromwell, the Catholics of Ireland had suffered greatly, but their faith remained strong. The legacy of these persecutions continued into the twentieth century and during the bloody new 'Troubles' within Northern Ireland during the 1970s, 80s and 90s.

All these factors fed into the unique period of the Restoration. It affected the governments and fledgling political movements and consequently into the English prejudice against Catholicism and later the Duke of York when he openly flaunted his conversion to Rome in 1676. With a lack of legitimate heirs from the king, the Exclusionists looked for viable Protestant alternatives to rule after Charles. These options included William of Orange and his wife Mary, as well as Monmouth. Monmouth would prove popular with the Exclusionists because he was of royal birth, albeit illegitimately, he was less foreign than William, although he was born in Rotterdam, and they thought he could be easily manipulated and used by the Exclusionists to achieve their political goals.

The main reason why there was an Exclusion Crisis to begin with was due to Charles II's inability to produce a legitimate heir with his wife, Catherine of Braganza. Monmouth was the eldest of seventeen recognised illegitimate children Charles had fathered with his numerous mistresses, who included the infamous Barbara Villiers, Countess of Castlemaine and 1st Duchess of Cleveland; the actress Nell Gwyn, and his French Catholic mistress Louise de Kérouaille, Duchess of Portsmouth, who was affectionately known as 'Fubbs'.

Queen Catherine was born in Alentejo, Portugal, on 25 November 1638. Her father would become King John IV (1 December 1640 to 6 November 1656) when the European super-dynasty of the Hapsburgs were deposed from the Portuguese throne in late 1640. Catherine subsequently became of equal royal status to Charles and made an excellent match for the then Prince of Wales. Negotiations regarding the royal match between the Houses of Stuart and Braganza started before the English Civil Wars, and would remain on hold during the brief republic under Oliver Cromwell and his parliamentarians.

The marriage between Catherine and Charles was not just about finding Charles a queen. The union also had European political support and, of course, financial benefits for the British treasury. The same hostilities that brought Catherine's father to the throne of Portugal were to encourage a partnership between the British throne and the new Portuguese royal family; ties to an established royal family through marriage would bring legitimacy and confidence to the new monarchy in Portugal. Both Britain and France wanted to support the new Portuguese royal house and saw the marriage as a way to aid Portugal while at the same time thwarting the Spanish Habsburgs.

Another reason why Charles required a wife was that she would bring a dowry and Catherine indeed brought a substantial sum to the union. Firstly, there was monetary value of £350,000, then there was the territory of Tangier in North Africa and lastly, the territory of Bombay in India. The Restoration court, notoriously known for its love of partying and opulence (a consequence of years in poverty in exile), was in great need of revenue and this dowry did a great deal to help relieve the cash flow problems and fill the nation's treasury.

Upon the Restoration, the marriage was finally agreed by Charles' Privy Council in May 1661, but not all of the court was happy with the match. Charles' mother is said to have preferred her son to have married a French queen instead.

It is highly unlikely that Charles undiplomatically exclaimed, 'Gentlemen, you have brought me a bat', making reference to his new wife's hair and clothes, which were styled in the Portuguese fashion. This would have been rude and cruel as well as politically awkward. If such words were ever uttered, Charles would no doubt have had the sense to make such observations away from the Portuguese diplomatic party as they presented the new queen to the court.

The great diarist of the Restoration, John Evelyn, also passed comment on the queen in a more favourable fashion:

> The Queen arrived with a train of Portuguese ladies in their monstrous fardingales, their complexions olivader [dark olive]

> and sufficiently unagreeable. Her Majesty in the same habit her fore-top long and turned aside strangely. She was yet of the hand somest countenance of all the rest and though low of stature prettily shaped, languishing and excellent eyes, her teeth wronging her mouth by sticking a little too far out; for the rest, lovely enough.[9]

Those words indicate that the new queen was of plain beauty rather than a traditional 'English rose', but still attractive in her exotic way. Samuel Pepys, another prominent diarist of the Restoration period, also described the queen in his journal stating,

> The Queene is brought a few days since to Hampton Court; and all people say of her to be a very fine and handsome lady and very discreet, and that the king is pleased enough with her: which I fear will put Madam Castlemaine's nose out of joynt.[10]

Charles continued to frolic with his mistresses after his marriage to Catherine, and only infrequently visited his marriage bed for relations to create an heir. The queen fell pregnant several times, but sadly all of the pregnancies ended in miscarriages. The first loss happened in 1666, four years after their marriage, a second miscarriage happened in 1668 and the last in 1669.

The dowry that made Catherine such a great match would also prove to be problematic. Between 1662 and 1663, about half of the sum had been paid to Charles, but the payments then stopped before restarting again in 1668. However, by 1680 only £243,000 (of the agreed £350,000) had been paid to the treasury. The Portuguese were slow in handing over the territory of Bombay and it only became British in 1665. Although Tangier was ideally placed in the Mediterranean, helping to give the Royal Navy dominance in that sea, the upkeep of this territory was approximately £55,000 per annum. The final insult to the British was when the Portuguese granted the British naval rivals, the Dutch, the same trading terms within the Portuguese empire as those granted to Britain. In the end, Catherine proved not to have been such a good match for Charles, politically, financially or as a queen consort.

If Charles had married another foreign princess then the fate of the Duke of Monmouth may well have been different, not to mention the course of British history, to the extent that the Stuart dynasty may not have ended with Queen Anne in 1714 and the subsequent arrival of the House of Hanover.

Chapter 5

The Private Life of a Public Duke

Monmouth was the eldest of Charles II's illegitimate children. The age difference between Monmouth and his half-siblings was quite large, meaning that during Charles' reign, Monmouth was more prominent within his father's court than any of his other half-siblings. This may have given the impression to some historical writers that Monmouth was his father's favourite child, but Charles was said to have been a warm and affectionate father and loved all his offspring equally. Having lost his own father and being unable to have legitimate children, just like any father, he only wanted to give any child of his the best opportunities in life, regardless of their illegitimate status. Royal bastards have always held a special place within royal courts, thus reinforcing the thought that Monmouth was no more special than his half-brothers and sisters.

In July 1662, just over two years after the Restoration, Dowager Queen Henrietta Maria brought her grandson, James, over to the English court at Charles' request. At this time he was twelve years old and was welcomed at Hampton Court as if he was a legitimate prince. A month later, James left the Tudor palace to join his father at the official royal court based at Whitehall.

There are numerous accounts describing the young Duke of Monmouth as the darling of the court, being well-liked and spoiled as if he was a prince. The scandal-loving royal observer and seventeenth-century socialite and diarist, Samuel Pepys, said the following of Monmouth at court in an entry dated 31 December 1662: 'The Duke of Monmouth is in so great splendour at Court, and dandled by the King, that some doubt that, if the King should have no child by the Queen, which there is yet no appearance of, whether he should not be acknowledged for a lawful son.'[11]

On 20 April 1663, Monmouth married Anne Scott, Duchess of Buccleuch. Anna, as she is sometimes referred to in primary documents, was the wealthiest heiress in Scotland and was born on 11 February 1651. Upon his marriage, James took his wife's surname of Scott which gave him an official surname for the first time in his life. Although Charles recognised him as

46

his son, he never legitimized him, meaning he was never legally a Stuart; according to the marriage contract, Monmouth was, *Filio nostro naturali et illegitimo,* (natural and illegitimate son). As his new wife, Anne was the party who brought money, wealth and estates to the marriage partnership, while James brought status through his new titles, the Duke of Monmouth, Orkney, Knight of the Garter, Earl of Doncaster and Baron Tynedale. Originally, the barony that he was to hold was to be that of Fotheringay, but Charles changed this to Tynedale due to Fotheringay's association with the execution of Mary Queen of Scots. The duke and duchess would have seven children in all; Isabella, Charles, James, Anne, Henry, Frances and Charlotte, four of whom died in childhood.

James came from an attractive gene pool. His mother, Lucy Walter has been described by John Evelyn as having 'Masses of dark chestnut hair, Sparkling eyes and a strange elfin, celtic [sic] quality about her'.[12] His father, Charles was tall, dark and handsome, although often described as the dark one of his siblings. He was also notoriously known as the 'Merry Monarch' for his success with the ladies. The fact he was the king may have had a role to play in his success with the fairer sex, but his dark, smouldering, dashing looks and charm would also have gone a long way in explaining why Charles acquired and seduced his many mistresses. Monmouth was a chip off the old block and just like his father, he was a Restoration ladies' man who had the added appeal of being a celebrated military hero, the son of a king, albeit an illegitimate one, and was a charming darling of the Restoration court.

The first of Monmouth's mistresses was Eleanor Needham. She was the daughter of Sir Robert Needham and was born in 1650. Their liaison started around 1674 and was to last about nine years. During this time the couple produced four children; James Crofts, Isabel Crofts, Henrietta Crofts and Henry Crofts. Monmouth provided his lover with a home on what is now Great Russell Street, in Bloomsbury, London. Soon after her last child to Monmouth was born, the duke's attention was taken by a new love interest.

Evidence of Monmouth's philandering can be found in a letter that forms part of Henry Sydney's Diary.

> The Duke of Monmouth has so little employment in state affairs that he has been at leisure … My Lady Wentworth's ill eyes did find cause, as she thought to carry her daughter into the countryside in so much haste that it makes a great noise, and done sure in some passion.[13]

This mention of the younger Lady Wentworth is more than mere scandalous gossip being passed around at court. Lady Henrietta Maria Wentworth would become an important influence and part of the last five years of Monmouth's life.

It is probable that Henrietta and Monmouth knew each other from court, as Lady Henrietta had been Maid of Honour to the Duchess of York. She was also cousin to Monmouth's guardian, Lord Crofts. There is evidence that the pair had definitely met each other by 1674 when they acted opposite one another in a play by John Crowns called *Calisto*. The play is also sometimes referred to as *The Chaste Nymph*. Monmouth played the part of the Shepherd and Henrietta Maria the part of Jupiter. At the time of the performance, Henrietta was fourteen years old, a very impressionable age for any young girl.

Henrietta's father, Thomas Wentworth, 1st Earl of Cleveland, was a prominent Cavalier during the Civil Wars and had been in charge of a cavalry wing during the Battle of Worcester in 1651. Wentworth would be taken prisoner a couple of times during the Civil Wars for his loyalty to the crown, first in 1644 and again in 1651 when he ended up in the Tower of London, where he was held until 1656. It was due to his time as a prisoner of war, his military services, as well as his loyalty to the Cavalier cause, that Wentworth was elevated socially and granted the peerage of the Earl of Cleveland in 1626. Cleveland should not be confused with his kin of the same name, Thomas Wentworth, 1st Earl of Strafford, who had been executed in 1645.

Henrietta Maria was Cleveland's only surviving heir and she took the title of Baroness Wentworth in her own right upon his death on 25 March 1667, but because Henrietta never produced a legitimate heir, the title has since become extinct.

By 1680 Henrietta Maria was twenty years old and reportedly was a beautiful, graceful young woman, with light brown hair and large, expressive eyes. It is at this time that the relationship between Monmouth and Henrietta became more than an infatuation. If their story had been written by Shakespeare they would have been star-crossed lovers. Monmouth, the married older man, dashing, charming, a military hero, the eldest son of a king, but sadly illegitimate and with limited prospects. Lady Wentworth, the young beautiful girl and the only heir to her deceased father's peerage and property, who was deeply and passionately in love with an unattainable man. He becomes a failed rebel and is tragically beheaded; she literally dies of a broken heart, having never recovered from his death.

The pair of lovers also seem to have had a joint interest in horoscopes. The notebook found on Monmouth when he was arrested had his horoscope drawn inside it, and there is a copy of Lady Wentworth's horoscope held in the Bodleian Library collection in Oxford.

Upon his banishment from court in 1683, following the discovery of the Rye House Plot, Monmouth fled to Toddington to be with his beloved Henrietta Maria. His time at Toddington seems to have been very happy and he wrote the following in his notebook about his time there:

> We'll to our bowers
> And there spend our hours
> Happy there we will be
> We no strifes there can see
> No Quarrelling for Crowns
> Nor fear the great ones frowns...
> We'll sit and bless our stars
> That this glorious place did give
> ...Did us Toddington give
> That thus we happy live.[14]

The extent of the passion between Monmouth and Henrietta can be seen most acutely at the end of their short and tragic lives. After Monmouth was banished indefinitely by his father at the end of 1683, he went to the Dutch Republic and Flanders where Henrietta Maria and her mother joined him. This is noted in correspondence between Chaloner Chute to the Countess of Rutland:

> The gracious Prince [Monmouth] is our neighbour here in Brussels and it is said here the Lady Harriot W[entworth] with him.[15]

The strength of their love was tested when they were asked to leave Brussels and found themselves having to seek shelter at the court of William of Orange and his wife, Mary. They had been asked to leave their home in Brussels because of the nature of their relationship living over the brush. Their non-marital status had been made known to the Catholic Marquis of Grana, who was the Governor of the Spanish Netherlands, which included Brussels. William and Mary, the Stadholders of the Dutch Republic, welcomed Monmouth and Henrietta to their court where they lived until Charles II's death. William's motivation for this may have been to send a message to his father-in-law, the Duke of York, as to where his and Mary's religious and political alliances lay; that is to say, with the Protestant Duke of Monmouth.

Monmouth was not the only one to be welcomed to the Orange court. Lady Henrietta was also well thought of, as can be seen here in a letter from the French ambassador to the Netherlands, Comte d'Avaux, to the Duke of York.

> The Princess of Orange has shown extraordinary marks of Honour to a young lady of quality from England who passes for the Duke of Monmouth's Mistress.[16]

This was a happy time for them both; they were part of the court and its entertainments, and living as a couple. This would all change in early 1685 upon the death of Monmouth's father.

No Rebellion can happen without funding. Monmouth received help from Henrietta Maria and her mother, both of whom sold most of their jewels and were able to raise the sum of £4,000 to give to the Duke: a lot of money to give a married man about to start a rebellion against his uncle, who happened to be the king of England. Henrietta Maria not only loved Monmouth deeply, but also firmly believed that he could overthrow his uncle and become the next Protestant king of England, despite the odds against him. This grand gesture is especially telling when you know that Monmouth's long suffering wife, Anne, impeded the sale of one of their properties, the Manor of Spalding, which could have provided Monmouth with an additional £10,000.[17] His wife clearly had less faith in his bid for the throne than his mistress. For her safety, Henrietta Maria and her mother stayed on the continent while Monmouth was engaged in fighting his rebellion.

Henrietta's story did not end well. She returned to England a month after the execution of her beloved Monmouth. Less than a year after Monmouth's execution, Baroness Henrietta Maria Wentworth breathed her last on 23 April 1686. She was buried at St George's Church, Toddington. Her tomb reads:

> Sacred to the memory of the right honourable Lady Henrietta, Baroness Wentworth who died unmarried April ye 23 1686. She was the sole daughter and heir of ye Right Honourable Thomas Lord Wentworth.

Many historians, particularly the military historians who have looked at the life and times of the Duke of Monmouth, have written out or reduced Henrietta Maria's role in Monmouth's life to a few lines or relegated her to the footnotes. According to the *Baronia Angelica Concentrata* compiled by Thomas Banks, the couple did have a child together, who like his father would have been illegitimate. At the time of his mother's death, their son was of the tender age of two years old and made the ward of Colonel Symth who 'brought him up as his own child and upon his decease left him his property and he assumed the name of his foster father and benefactor.'[18] There are many reasons why Monmouth took the actions he did, but we should not underestimate the influence of the woman he adored, a woman who had a great passion, love and ambition for her man.

Chapter 6

The Making of a Military Man

The Duke of Monmouth was a man of action, who during his military career accomplished an outstanding military record within the British, French and Dutch armies. The duke started his military career in 1665 aged just sixteen years old, when he served in the Royal Navy under his uncle and future rival for the throne, James, Duke of York, during the Second Anglo-Dutch War.

On 3 June 1665, the Dutch fleet attacked off the cost of Lowestoft. The Duke of York won the battle and it was a great victory for the young Monmouth to observe. Three years later, on 4 January 1670, Monmouth was made Colonel of the King's Life Guard; a very senior appointment within the army for someone aged only nineteen. In the following year, he took the post of Captain General of the Army, which had become available after the death of the 1st Duke of Albemarle, George Monck. This rapid rise through the armed forces, with very little first-hand military experience, caused exasperation and disquiet within the Country faction of parliament. Although it was not unusual for high offices within the army to be filled by nobility, his age and the fact that he was the king's illegitimate son would not have made Monmouth popular with this section of the political classes.

The Third Anglo-Dutch War started in April 1672, when England and France went to war against the Dutch. The English excuse for declaring war on their fellow Protestant nation was flimsy: on 24 August 1671, a Dutch ship did not salute their flag towards a British ship, the *Merlin*, within British waters. Charles, encouraged by his Privy Council, demanded that the admiral of the Dutch ship should be punished for the lack of respect shown to the British ship. Unsurprisingly, the Dutch administration within The Hague refused to punish their admiral for such a minor offence. This in turn gave Charles the excuse he required to join the war and keep Louis happy, as well as fulfilling the terms of the Secret Treaty of Dover between Britain and France.

The Duke of Monmouth would have irritated the future Whig party further by taking part in the campaign against the Dutch Republic in 1672,

The Execution of Charles I (artist unknown, c.1649). The execution of Monmouth's grandfather, Charles I, was important because the political and social repercussions affected the politics of the Restoration during Monmouth's lifetime.

Portrait of Oliver Cromwell, Lord Protectorate of the Commonwealth of Britain by Gaspar de Crayer (early 17th century). Cromwell helped revolutionise the standing army through training and discipline and led the country through the republican years under the grand title of Lord Protector. His signature appears third on Charles I's death warrant.

Left: Henrietta Maria of France, Queen of England, by Anthony Van Dyke. Monmouth's paternal grandmother, Henrietta Maria, was a formidable Catholic matriarch who cared for Monmouth until 1662.

Below: Charles II by Henri Gascar (17th century). Monmouth's father and greatest ally until 1683. Monmouth greatly resembled Charles, inheriting his dark colouring and charming personality.

Portrait of James, Duke of York, later James II, by John Michael Wright (1660-65). York was Monmouth's biggest rival during Charles II's lifetime. After the king's death, Monmouth's Uncle James became his biggest nemesis.

Image taken from a Jacobite broadsheet depicting Anne, Duchess of Monmouth with her sons (c.1715). Monmouth's long-suffering wife was faithful to him until the end.

Left: Equestrian portrait of James Scott, 1st Duke of Monmouth (artist unknown, mid 17th century). Monmouth the military hero, in the thick of the action – as he should be remembered.

Below: Illustration of the Maastricht Siege, engraved by Iollain (c.1675). During the siege, Monmouth impressed his royal, French cousin, Louis XIV, with his military strategy and was richly rewarded for his bravery.

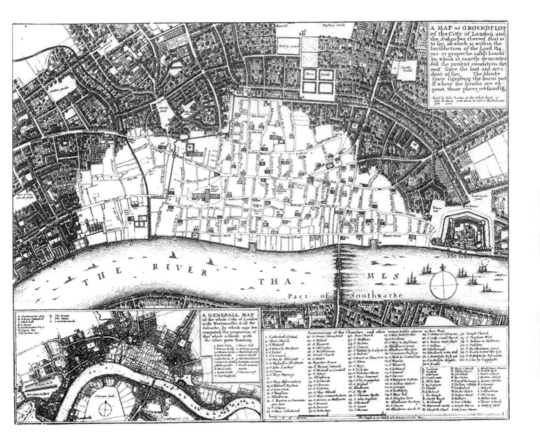

A map by Wenceslas Hollar (c.1666-7) showing the destroyed areas of London after the Great Fire in 1666.

Portrait of Anthony Ashley Cooper, Earl of Shaftesbury, by John Greenhill (c.1672-73). Shaftesbury was the first 'modern' politician and a leading figure in the Exclusion Crisis, as well as being an early Whig MP.

Portrait of John Locke by Sir Godfrey Kneller (1697). Locke was Shaftesbury's personal physician and a member of his household, who shared and influenced his politics.

Woodcut of Titus Oates by Thomas Hawker (mid 17ᵗʰ century). Oates was the inventor of the Popish Plot, which created the ideal political climate for the Exclusion policy to thrive, thus setting Protestants against Catholics.

Monmouth's interview with James II, by John Pettie (1882). Monmouth is seen grovelling for clemency from his uncle, James II.

Portrait of George Jeffreys of Wem, by William Wolfgang Claret (c.1678-80).
Jeffreys was the ruling judge during the trials of Monmouth's rebels, in what
became known as the Bloody Assizes.

where his regiment marched 'two thousand very good men and in good order.'[19] English involvement in the conflict only lasted until 1674, while Louis XIV continued to fight the Dutch until 1678.

King Louis XIV was so impressed with Monmouth's performance in the war that on 31 January 1673, at St Germain, the French King presented him with valuable gifts including a diamond ring worth 17,500 livres and a sword set with diamonds worth an additional 38,000 livres. In April the same year, Louis further honoured Monmouth when he created him a Lieutenant General and granted him an allowance towards the costs of his appointment.

During 1673, Monmouth became the Lord Lieutenant of the East Riding of Yorkshire. He was also made the Governor of Kingston-Upon-Hull. The duke was held in such esteem that in 1674 he would also be made Chancellor of Cambridge University, a great honour considering he was not a former scholar of the university. The honours bestowed upon him did not stop there; he was also created the Lord Lieutenant of Staffordshire. To be awarded such positions, honorary or not, would have meant that he had gained a prodigious reputation in his own right – because although he was of royal decent, he was still a bastard.

It was during the Siege of Maastricht that Monmouth's achievements would help to galvanise his reputation as a promising military leader. The siege itself was part of the French strategy against the Dutch in their ongoing war. Maastricht was a strategically well-placed fortified town within Flanders. The area of Flanders is an ambiguous name given to territories that now lie within the modern boarders of Belgium, France and the Netherlands. In the summer of 1673, Louis XIV and his French army found themselves having problems resourcing supplies for their army. The capture of the fortified city of Maastricht would help alleviate this strategical problem of unreliable sources of supplies and would allow Catholic France to continue to wage war against the Protestant Dutch provinces more effectively.

In mid-June 1673, the French started their attack on the walled city. They fired cannon at the fortified walls of Maastricht, in the hope of weakening them. This tactic was then followed by men digging irregular trenches in a zigzag pattern, so that the men at the top of the Maastricht fort would have difficulty in locating and hitting the French soldiers. Additionally, this tactic gave the French soldiers rudimentary protection from what was being fired on them from the defences of the fortification, as well as to allow men to tunnel towards the base of the fortification so that they could lay explosives in the hope of weakening the walls of the city from below. Louis was so confident these tactics would work that he was hoping that he would be able to celebrate Catholic mass in Maastricht Cathedral, on the feast of St John the Baptist on 24 June.

During this part of the siege, some of the French military did manage to breach the fort. The fighting would not last for long though, and the Duke of Monmouth played a key role in what happened at Maastricht, displaying a remarkable tactical grasp throughout the operation and *une conduite d'un general qui auorit commandé 30 ans tranchées.*[*]

Many of the French that had managed to breach Maastricht's city walls had been pushed back, not by the Dutch but the Spanish. The Spanish were on the side of the Dutch even though they were a Catholic nation. They were rivals with the French as well as having territories within the Dutch Provinces. So although Spain's primary reason for entering the war was to protect their territories, it also afforded them a good opportunity to clash with their rival, France.

During the conflict, Monmouth had been fighting for the French, as the commander of an English regiment of 6,000 men. The Secret Treaty of Dover was the reason why Charles sent Monmouth and his men to fight against fellow Protestants, despite the fact that both parliament and popular opinion was against aiding the French against the Dutch. After the French had been pushed back, morale among Monmouth's men dropped and there were deserters. The situation did not look good. It was Monmouth, with a young John Churchill (the future Duke of Marlborough), who would lead a second assault on the city. Churchill would later go on to have one of the most accomplished military and political careers of the late seventeenth and early eighteenth centuries, spanning the reigns of the last five monarchs of the Stuart house. Although fighting for the same cause during the siege of Maastricht, Churchill and Monmouth would find themselves on opposite sides during Monmouth's rebellion in 1685.

Louis XIV informed his royal cousin, Charles II, of his son's brave actions at Maastricht when he wrote that '[Monmouth had] attacked their guard in hand upon the first alarm of the sortie,... and dislodged them.'[20] To have been noticed and mentioned by the French king was an honour and testament to Monmouth's skill as a military leader, who showed great bravery in action. The siege ended in a victory for the French, and Monmouth was credited with playing a major role in the eventual outcome.

The following year on 21 August 1674, the siege was re-enacted for the entertainment of King Charles and his court on a meadow close to the Long

---

[*] 'the conduct of a general who had spent 30 years in the trenches'.

Terrace at Windsor Castle. John Evelyn was there to see the spectacle and wrote the following on the event:

> Greate gunns fir'd on both sides, granados shot, mines sprung, parties sent out, attempts of raising the siege, prisoners taken, parleys, and in short all the circumstances of a formal siege to appearance and, what is most strange, do without disorder or ill accident to the great satisfaction of a thousand spectators.[21]

However, by 1678, despite all the praise and accolades bestowed on him by Louis, Monmouth had changed sides and was now fighting in an alliance with the Dutch against the French. During the closing stages of the Franco-Dutch War, Monmouth commanded an Anglo-Dutch brigade and was said to have distinguished himself once again in battle; his change of allegiance did more harm to his father's relationship with Louis than to his own military or personal reputation.

Monmouth encapsulated and represented in so many ways, through his heritage and military career, all that the fledgling Whig Party thought was wrong with Charles and his hedonistic and opulent court. However, it was his Protestant faith, his royal heritage (regardless of its illegitimate status), his change of allegiance in the Franco-Dutch conflict, and his impressionable and charming personality that would draw him to the attention of Shaftesbury and the budding Whig Party, who would see Monmouth as a more suitable alternative to the current heir to the throne.

On 22 June 1679, the Battle of Bothwell Bridge took place after an accumulation of religious and political tensions that had been simmering since the restoration of Charles II. It shows the Duke of Monmouth at his military best, demonstrating how he was able to manipulate this success and make himself a Protestant Anglican military hero; an image he would use to full advantage in the coming years, in the run up to his rebellion in 1685.

The Presbyterians in Scotland, although Protestant, were considered nonconformist and were, like the Quakers, Baptist and Methodists penalised under the law just like the Catholics after the restoration of Charles in 1660. The Scottish Presbyterians would meet in open spaces to preach to their congregations and these 'illegal' gatherings would frequently be broken up by government troops. The head of these religious rebels was Robert Hamilton of Preston.

Monmouth had been deployed to Scotland by his father due to a number of skirmishes there that had threatened to cause unrest and might possibly turn into a Scottish rebellion, or worse, a new civil war. He was accompanied north with 5,000 troops in order to quash the infant insurrection and prevent it from spilling over the border into England.

On 22 June the rebels, led by Robert Hamilton, numbered an estimated 6,000 men, as opposed to Monmouth's 5,000. Although they had more men, they were not militarily trained or disciplined like the force Monmouth had brought north with him; one of the civil war legacies was that it had introduced well-trained armed forces to defend the nation. Monmouth also had support from the Viscount of Dundee and the Earl of Linlithgow.

The battle was centred on a narrow bridge across the river Clyde, which gave its name to the battle. Monmouth's success was mostly due to the fact that he was able to take control of the bridge, thus making the rebels on the other side easier to rout. The casualty numbers for the rebels seems to range between 500-700 men and approximately 1,200 soldiers were taken prisoner. There were comparatively very few deaths among Monmouth's men; skill, discipline experience, good leadership and an element of luck meaning that very few lost their lives. A letter from Henry Coventry to the Marquis of Ormond provides details of the battle and Monmouth:

> Since the last to you by the express I have little more to add, only there is a confirmation come from the Duke of Monmouth of the defeat, seven or eight hundred killed upon the place and about twelve hundred prisoners brought to Edinburgh.[22]

The Protestant Covenanters that were taken hostage by the royal forces, led by Monmouth, were taken and then held in gaol in Edinburgh. In November 1679, the prisoners that had survived the harsh conditions of their time in captivity, were then transported to the colonies as punishment for their rebellious behaviour.

The Battle of Bothwell Bridge shows Monmouth as a competent and successful military leader on his home turf. Memories and tales of successes like this would have helped encourage men to follow him in six years later into treasonous rebellion against his uncle James.

The battle also meant that Monmouth won favours within the Court alliance for defending Anglicanism. Somewhat ironically, he also politically irritated the Country faction of the House of Commons, who would later transform into the Whigs, which would emerge as his champion. They found the quashing of any Protestant minority uncomfortable. It can also provide an insight into Monmouth's personality. Many military commanders would have treated their prisoners of war with less humanity, but instead of mass execution they were transported.

In an exchange that was said to have taken place at Windsor between Charles and his son upon the latter's return to court following his victory in Scotland, the king was said to have accused Monmouth of being too kind towards the prisoners. In his reply, Monmouth declared that he was incapable of killing men in cold blood, declaring that that was work only for a butcher.[23]

The attitude of Monmouth towards unnecessary killing would also cast doubt over his involvement within the Rye House Plot, for it would be a cold blooded and ruthless man that would plot to kill and assassinate his own father and king. Monmouth was a military man and killing was part of his job, however, only it would seem when necessary. Had Charles started to distrust his son? Could Monmouth's compassion and leniency towards his prisoners from the Battle of Bothwell Bridge have been a political move to endear himself to the Scottish populace, in the same way he would try when he undertook progresses around the country in the following year? This would be the last time that Monmouth was not seen as a blatant predatory threat to his uncle, the Duke of York, as an alternative heir to the throne.

Chapter 7

The Catholic Threat

The two James, the Dukes of York and Monmouth, may not have been close, but they were family and both shared a joint love of Charles. It was Charles' love for each of them that caused him to make the difficult decision to first exile York and then later Monmouth. Unfortunately, the exiles did not achieve what Charles had hoped. Instead of reducing the political focus on either duke, sending first York and then Monmouth away from the politics of London to Europe, it only exaggerated anti-Catholic focus on York and encourage pro-Exclusionist focus towards Monmouth.

When Monmouth was born, York was one of the few at court who did not believe that the little boy was Charles' offspring. This belief was soon dismissed as the young Monmouth grew up. Indeed, all of the doubters had to change their minds as the little boy looked just like his father had done at the same age. This might have been why his grandmother was very fond of the young Monmouth. After the Restoration when Monmouth arrived at court as a teenager, the two dukes lived cheek-by-jowl within Charles' libertine court. However, it seems from this early stage that the two Jameses were certainly only tolerant of each other.

Samuel Pepys observed the three royals together and recorded the following in his diary on 26 July 1665:

> The King having dined, he came down and I went in the barge with him, I sitting at the door hearing him and the Duke [York] talk … they are both princes of great nobleness and spirits. The Duke of Monmouth is most skittish, leaping gallant that ever I saw, always in action, vaulting or leaping or clambering.[24]

Whether the two dukes liked it or not, they were living together within the royal court and would have to learn to tolerate each other if they wished to maintain a good relationship with the king.

The Dukes of York and Monmouth had to work together during the Anglo-Dutch Wars. Therefore, in the second such conflict in 1665, a fresh faced and green sixteen-year-old Monmouth served under his uncle, the Admiral of the Royal Navy, upon the flagship, the *Royal Charles*. On 3 June, Monmouth experienced his first naval battle off Lowestoft when the *Royal Charles* was hit in the quarterdeck, frightfully close to where Monmouth was standing. The duke was lucky to emerge unharmed as several men who were close to him, including Lords Falmouth and Muskerry, were killed when the deck was hit.

The Secret Treaty of Dover saw King Charles promise Louis XIV military support against the Dutch in exchange for a pension, the two dukes found themselves working with the French in the Third Anglo-Dutch War in 1672. This time, Monmouth led a small brigade of British troops, as part of the French army, having proved his military ability. Meanwhile, the Duke of York commanded the British naval force to support the French against the Dutch Republic. The fact that Monmouth was not at his uncle's side and fighting with the navy during this conflict was probably because he had shown greater skills as a military leader while serving as a colonel of the King's Life Guard, rather than because he simply did not like his uncle York. Monmouth was therefore able to serve his father and the French better on the ground than in his uncle's shadow.

Charles hoped that by removing the Duke of York from immediate political focus by asking him to leave the country for a while, this would improve the political situation and maybe help towards healing relations between his son and brother. This exile from court and country in 1679 must have frustrated and angered York as he was the legal heir to the throne; it must have seemed to him that Charles was favouring his illegitimate son. James set sail for the Dutch Republic on 3 March 1679 under the pretence of visiting his daughter, Mary and her husband, William of Orange. However, York was returned from his unofficial exile from Europe when, in August of the same year, Charles fell dangerously ill. York arrived at Windsor Castle on 2 September 1679 much to the despondence of Monmouth, who York recorded in a handwritten note as being 'sort of disorder and disturb'd carriage in him.'[25] upon discovering his uncle's return.

Once the king had recovered from his illness, he again tried to resolve the political and family tensions by sending both his beloved son and then his brother and heir into exile again. The Duke of Monmouth also lost his military posts, as well as being banished from the country.

Monmouth's fall from military office was recorded by Charles Hatton, the younger brother of Viscount Hatton: 'The Duke of Monmouth is turned out of all command and banished the three kingdoms. This day he has gone to Windsor to surrender his patents.'[26]

In turn, the Duke of York wrote to his son-in-law, William of Orange, gloating of the disgrace of his rival and nephew, Monmouth:

> Though it may make the Duke of Monmouth ... More popular amongst the ill men and seditious people [it] will quite dash his foolish hopes that he so vainly pursued. This his Majesty resolved in, upon it being represented to him that it was not reasonable to leave the Duke of Monmouth here and send me back again to Flanders.[27]

The Duke of York seemed to have been the opposite to his brother Charles in personality. Charles was charming, personable, witty, charismatic and popular, whereas the Duke of York comes across as stiff, formal, impatient, stubborn, hot-headed, pompous and not well liked either in court or by the people. Both Charles and York faced powerful political opposition. Where Charles employed patience and subterfuge, York sought open confrontation fuelled by arrogance and a biased passion for his beliefs. The most obvious example of this can be seen in his behaviour surrounding his conversion to Rome. He deliberately converted despite the fact that he knew that such an action would cause problems for both his brother, as well as himself as the heir to the throne. His self-righteous attitude and arrogance, so like his father's, made him think that parliament's opinions and those of the people he was going to rule were unimportant. It was this attitude that would make York, once he was King James II, a dangerous opponent for Monmouth and why Monmouth and his rebellion had to succeed if he was to defeat his uncle. Unfortunately, Monmouth did not win and his uncle was never going to show Monmouth any mercy; it was not in his personality to be forgiving, merciful or compassionate.

Of course, there are two sides to every story and Monmouth did not exactly make himself likeable to his uncle James. Although he could not help the situation of his birth or his parentage, he could have lived a more private life, just like his half-siblings had managed to do. Instead, he was easily led by manipulative men with political motives and agendas. He fell for their flattery and encouraged him to believe that he could become king. He would become entangled in various schemes, with plotters encouraging him to undertake progresses similar to those embarked upon by monarchs. This association and behaviour only made him threatening to York and meant he was seen as a real danger. It was also the start of his path towards treason, rebellion and ultimately his date with death, on Tower Hill.

The Great Fire of London was one of the major historical events of the seventeenth century. A major consequence of the fire would be the subsequent modernising of the city. Due to the location of the fire, the majority of the buildings engulfed by the flames were the dilapidated medieval wooden slums. The fire was also subsequently responsible for launching the career of the most successful English architect of the century, Sir Christopher Wren, who as a result will forever be associated with the rebuilding of London and the most momentous achievement of his life's work, St Paul's Cathedral.

The fire started on Sunday 2 September 1666, in Pudding Lane, East London within a small bakery that belonged to Mr Thomas Farriner. The statistics associated with the fire are both surprising and shocking. Firstly, considering location of where the fire started, as well as the parts of London that were destroyed by the blaze, only six people were officially recorded as losing their lives due to the fire. Realistically, this figure is probably higher, as the poor who inhabited the slums prior to the outbreak of the fire, would have been highly unlikely to report the death of a family member when most of them had already lost everything they owned. Survival rather than bureaucracy was more important in the immediate aftermath of this disaster for the poorest.

Eighty-seven parish churches within the east of London were destroyed in the fire. The biggest of these churches to have been lost was the old St Paul's Cathedral. Some may have said that the loss of the old cathedral may have been a blessing as it was in a woefully poor state of repair for such an important place of worship.

Of the 80,000 homes within the area affected by the fire, 70,000 were destroyed; either by the flames or as a preventive measure to stop the spread of the blaze going any further. The loss of so many homes meant that there was a very large number of displaced people, still in their own city, with no property to their name. If you assume that each home held five people that means at least 350,000 people with nowhere to go and nothing but the clothes on their back, unless they were one of the lucky few who managed to save some of their possessions before their homes were engulfed by the flames. That is 350,000 people requiring water, shelter, food and sanitation at the very basic level. It is also worth remembering that some of these slums would have housed far more people that five, so the number of displaced persons would have probably been more than the conservative estimate above. The Great Fire would continue its destructive path, engulfing London until Wednesday 5 September.

The fire had repercussions for the story of the Duke of Monmouth, as well as the history and cityscape of London. The primary reason it affected Monmouth's future is due to what the London mob would perceive to be the cause of the fire and how it was subsequently manipulated by the Exclusionists for their cause. The Great Fire was also used by the agitator Titus Oates as anti-Catholic propaganda during the Popish Plot to reinforce his lies and turn public feeling against the Duke of York.

Thomas Farriner, the owner of the bakery in Pudding Lane, also held the court title of Conduct of the King's Bakehouse. This title gave him the honour of supplying both the Palace of Whitehall with its daily bread, as well as the Royal Navy with sea biscuits. As well as the prestige of the title, the position would also have given him a steady and regular source of income. The baker was never charged with deliberately starting the fire and he would continue baking and trading until his death four years later, in 1670.

As early as 5 September, on the third and final day of the fire, while the flames were dying, the people of London were already blaming the French for the disaster, as Samuel Pepys notes in his diary: 'discourse now began that there is a plot in it and that the French had done it'.[28] One of the reasons that the London mob would firmly blame the fire on a French Catholic conspiracy was due to the fact that a delusional and mentally unstable Frenchman would falsely confess to starting the blaze.

The individual was a twenty-six-year-old watchmaker from Rouen, Normandy, named Robert Hubert. When questioned, Hubert's confession changed and contradicted itself several times during the different interrogations, as well as at his trial. He claimed that he and an individual called Stephen Piedloe were acting as French spies and were recruited for the job in Paris. He claimed that he, with the help of other men, were carrying out orders direct from the Pope. These orders were to burn the heathen Protestant city of London along with its scandalous and libertine court. The number of people Hubert claimed to have helped him in his plan changed each time he retold his confession. Hubert claimed that he and Piedloe arrived in the city on 1 September 1666 and waited until nightfall before going to Pudding Lane where they proceeded to set fire to the bakery with the aid of fireballs. He had apparently been paid one gold coin and been promised four more coins for his trouble upon his return to France, having successfully burnt down the city of London and the royal court. Strangely, the mysterious Stephen Piedloe was never found, assuming that he ever existed.

Other inconsistencies within Hubert's story included the fact he claimed to be Catholic when he was in fact a French Huguenot Protestant. The number of 'fireballs' he claimed to have used to set the bakery alight altered, so did the dates he claimed to have arrived in London, as well as where the ship he sailed in, the *Skipper*, actually docked in London. In fact, the Skipper arrived in London two days after the fire had started. The strangest lie Hubert told was that he actually threw fireballs at the bakery in Pudding Lane. This was physically impossible for Hubert to do, as he had a physical handicap that would not have enabled him to carry out such an action. Even at his trial in October 1666, nobody fully believed his story or comprehended why he was confessing to committing this capital crime. However, due to the fact that he had confessed in a court of law, the court was legally obliged to find him guilty and convict him of the crime of treason, which in turn carried the death penalty. He was subsequently executed at Tyburn on 29 October, fifty-six days after the fire started. Many hoped that the conviction of a 'foreign' scapegoat would help to settle some of the tension that had developed in London.

The Earl of Clarendon, who was also the Lord Chancellor at the time of the Great Fire, described the tragic Hubert as a 'poor distracted wretch, weary of his life and choose to part with it this way.'[29] Indeed, Hubert may have felt in his final days that he had finally achieved something in his life, through the fame and notoriety he gained for falsely confessing to this crime.

This conviction of the Frenchman Robert Hubert would be reinforced later with a scathing inscription added on the base of the Monument, erected in remembrance of the Great Fire, with the following words, 'But Popish frenzy which wrought such horrors, is not yet quenched'. This was inscribed on the north-facing panel in 1681, only to be re-inscribed minus the anti-Catholic quotation during the short reign of James II. The lines would be re-added again by his daughter Mary and her husband William of Orange. The anti-Catholic words would remain on the plinth until Catholic emancipation in 1829. Most importantly though, these words were there to remind the Protestant mob during the Exclusion Crisis of the potential dangers of a Catholic inheriting the throne.

There was already an appetite for anti-Catholicism within the political establishment before the Exclusion Crisis took hold of politics in the early 1680s. This can be most keenly seen in the passing of the discriminatory

Test Acts of 1672 & 1678. These acts were aimed at Catholic members of Parliament, the first Test Act excluded the House of Lords from its terms as well as those who held posts within the armed forces. The Duke of York, who was the Admiral of the Royal Navy, would now become affected by the passing of these prejudiced acts. Each member of parliament and person of military office had to swear an oath renouncing the Catholic belief of Transubstantiation. The oath needed to be sworn in front of a witness and was as follows:

> I X, do declare that I do believe that there is not any transubstantiation in the sacrament of the Lord's Supper, or in the elements of the Bread and Wine, at or after the Consecration thereof by any person whatsoever.

The Earl of Shaftesbury, together with the Duke of Monmouth, fulfilled the requirements of the Test Act together at the London church of St Clement the Danes, with John Locke as their witness.

As Transubstantiation is the central belief of all practising Catholics who held their faith as important, those who did believe it would not have been able to swear this oath for fear of their immortal soul. They would have had to resign their seats in the House of Commons or their posts within the Army or Royal Navy. The Exclusionists would later argue that if the Duke of York was unable to hold the lesser office of Admiral of the Navy due to his religious conviction, he was not suitable to inherit the throne as it required him, as monarch, to become the figurehead of the Anglican Church.

The act was amended during the height of the Popish Plot in 1678 so that members of House of Lords also had to swear the oath. This change came about as five Catholic Lords had become embroiled in the scheming lies of the profligate Titus Oates. The Test Acts therefore show that there was strong anti-Catholic feeling before the policy of Exclusion was brought before parliament in the hope of becoming the law.

The Clarendon Codes, just like the discriminatory Test Acts, were legally passed during the Restoration parliament, allowing a person to be discriminated against based on their religious beliefs and practices, and took their name from Charles II's first minister, Edward Hyde, Earl of Clarendon. However, the name of the laws is somewhat misleading as Clarendon was not the instigator or composer of these deplorable acts, nor did he even agree with most of the content of the statutes that bear his name.

There were a total of four acts that would made up the Clarendon Codes and they were: The Corporation Act (1661); The Act of Uniformity (1662); The Conventicle Act (1664) and the Five Mile Act (1665). Although all four acts would prejudice against non-Anglican Protestants, also known as nonconformists, it is the first two acts of the code that most interest us here. Nonconformist Protestant sects and groups included Quakers, Calvinists, Methodists, Anabaptists, Lutherans, Baptists and Puritans.

The Corporation Act, passed in 1661, only a year into the reign of Charles II, was similar to the later Test Acts as it ensured that nonconformist Protestants were unable to hold office, military or civil. Additionally, nonconformist Christians were prohibited to gain qualifications from Oxford and Cambridge universities. The law also meant that those of nonconformist beliefs were forced to reject The Solemn League; the bargain drawn up between the Kirk and Parliamentarians during the Civil Wars to reform the English Church in line with Presbyterianism.

Just as the Test Act wanted Catholics to denounce the Transubstantiation, this code demanded that the nonconformists give up the freedom to worship as they wished. This made the legitimate alternative heir to Charles, William of Orange, less agreeable as he was not part of the Anglican church, but instead a nonconformist Calvinist.

The second code of importance was the Act of Uniformity. The law reinforced that the Anglican Common Book of Prayer was the only religious text to be used during the celebration of religious ceremonies and was the only book of prayer to be taught in all educational institutions, from parish schools to the highest universities in the land. These laws were made to ensure that England was not only Protestant, but practised a very English form of Protestantism. Monmouth was the very embodiment of this and it was something that the Exclusionists encouraged and used as propaganda while the duke was progressing around the country in 1681 and 1683.

The Secret Treaty of Dover was also the cause of further division. Formed of two parts, the first was a secret treaty that was signed in the summer of 1670, while the second part was in effect a cover-up document signed during December of that year. The men chosen to put their names to this agreement, in December 1670, were the Catholic members of the Cabal group. These documents negotiated a controversial agreement between King Charles II and his French cousin, King Louis XIV.

The Treaty of Dover was brought to the English court by Charles' youngest sister, Henrietta Anne, affectionately known as Minette. She was the Duchess of Orleans and sister-in-law to Louis XIV, although there were rumours she was also his mistress.

Within the terms of this treaty, Charles agreed to change his faith to Roman Catholicism, to support France in their grievances with their rivals, the Spanish, and lastly give military support to France against the Dutch. In return for complying to the terms of the treaty, Charles would receive a pension from Louis to keep him independent from his problematic parliament and access to additional troops for when he converted to Roman Catholicism.

Charles may have seen that by confirming the Catholic Duke of York as his heir, it was his way of returning his nation to Catholicism. By doing this, Charles himself would be spared the political upheaval and unrest of openly converting to Rome and that any public backlash or possible uprising would happen after his death. We know that he may have wanted to convert to Rome and may have even confided this to Louis, however, he would wait until he was on his deathbed before finally becoming a Catholic.

Throughout his reign, Charles constantly showed opposition to laws passed by his government that persecuted Catholics, especially those within public and civil service offices. Many of his trusted advisers were Catholic and he saw their persecution as the government's way of curtailing his power. It is possible that he may have only agreed to this secret Catholic clause as a way of pleasing his sister Minette, and that he had no intention of converting to Rome during his reign. In fact, he may have been playing a Machiavellian stratagem; by not converting he was keeping Louis dangling and in theory, ensuring a steady supply of money. In equal measure, it may also be that the treaty would only have meant that Charles, not the nation, would have changed faith. This may be missing the point. The populace's understanding of Catholicism at the time was that it meant autocratic rule. It was more than a personal choice of faith; it was a threat to stability, politically and religiously, as well as a grim reminder of the reign of Charles I and its eventual consequences.

The main reason that Charles willingly entered into and signed the clandestine treaty was that he required money, and Louis was offering him generous sums so that he wouldn't need to call Parliament. Parliament manipulated Charles' need for money as a way of bending him to their will, by making him sign laws they knew he would not ordinarily agree to, such as the Test Acts. As well as converting back to Rome and bringing England with him, Charles also agreed within the terms of the treaty to help Louis in his war against the Dutch Republic.

The Dutch Republic, at the time of this treaty, were in the middle of what would became known as their Golden Age, when they were at the height of their successful trade and empire that was maintained by their strong navy. They were also at the peak of their most influential artistic and cultural period; many influential Dutch masters emerged at this time, including Pieter de Hooch and Johannes Vermeer. They were also one of the most religiously tolerant nations in Europe; as long as you worked hard, how you communed with your God was of no matter to the Dutch state.

Because they were fellow Protestants, the Dutch Republic should have been a natural ally to Britain, especially as they were also an imperial and naval power. Additionally, Charles' nephew, William of Orange and his niece, Mary Stuart were the Stadtholders in the region. However, Louis XIV was offering Charles something the Dutch were not: money. The Third Anglo-Dutch War would come about as a direct result of the Treaty of Dover. The conflict also enabled Monmouth to show his military ability and experience within an English brigade as part of the French army. The rest of the military support the British offered the French was through naval defence, under the command of the Duke of York.

The treaties of Dover were important to Monmouth's fate as they led Charles into war against the Dutch United Provinces and established him firmly on the side of the French. This in turn caused people to perceive that he might be in league with Catholic France; which of course he was, albeit secretly. This in turn increased general feelings of animosity and suspicion towards the Duke of York and the possibility of him inheriting the throne. The consequences of the Treaty of Dover became useful for the Exclusionist's cause as they manipulated these growing anti-Catholic fears within society.

Restoration London was a highly-politicised society, with politics and news being shared and debated within the city's new coffee shops. Upon entering these exclusively male establishments, the customers were greeted with, 'What news?' Pamphlets, printed with news and gossip from the court and country, were available for the patrons to read along with early forms of newspapers known as news sheets. The best-known and still surviving of these publications is the *London Gazette*, although today it is used to announce legal notices such as bankruptcies and commercial liquidations.

The Green Ribbon Club was just one of many political clubs that were emerging in London at this time. It was frequented by MPs, mainly from the Country faction of Parliament and their hangers on, and they held their gatherings near the Inns of Court at the King's Head tavern on Chancery Lane. The name of the inn they choose for their meeting venue was appropriately named, as many of the members of the club were former Cromwellian supporters, disgruntled with the Restoration court and its lax and licentious behaviour and pro-Catholic stance. During the meetings, the disgruntled members would discuss, debate, drink and plot when Parliament had been dissolved at the whim of Charles II.

Eventually, the members became known as the Green Ribbon Club after they took to wearing hats trimmed with green ribbon and adorned with accompanying green ribbon corsages. The motif of a green ribbon is suggestive of the club's political leanings and ideas, as green ribbons were worn by the Levellers during the Civil Wars.

Given the nature of the meetings and the topics of conversation and debate, there is little surprise in the names of some of their members. They included Lords Bedford, Buckingham, Cavendish, Halifax, Macclesfield and Shaftesbury. Titus Oates of the Popish Plot notoriety and even Monmouth was one of their attendees. Another interesting member was John Claypole; Oliver Cromwell's son-in-law.

The Green Ribbon Club was not just a drinking club that fuelled plots, it was also the birth of political stratagem and activism.

> The Whigs met in London coffee houses and in the Green Ribbon Club ... They orchestrated a lurid press campaign - made possible after the Licensing Act lapsed ... to influence the October elections. Their reward was a House of Commons solidly behind their programme of Exclusion.[30]

In John Dryden's epic political poem *Absalom and Achitophel,* he describes Shaftesbury as Achitophel. The malcontents of the Israelites were the Exclusionists, with Achitophel the leader helping to unite them to achieve the 'same design'; the exclusion of the Duke of York. This was exactly what happened within the Green Ribbon Club; it allowed the Exclusionists to plot and plan.

> To farther this Achitophel unites
> The malcontents of all the Israelites:
> Whose differing parties he could wisely join,
> For several ends, to serve the same design.

The fortunes of the Green Ribbon Club were tied to that of the Exclusionists and the early Whigs. With the discovery of the Rye House assassination plot, which caused Shaftesbury to flee to the continent, the Green Ribbon Club lost their effective leadership. After the fall of the Duke of Monmouth, their ideal Protestant figurehead, the Green Ribbon Club declined and eventually dissolved during James II's reign.

Chapter 8

The Popish Plot

Titus Oates was the fantasist who fabricated the Popish Plot for unknown reasons. Oates most likely created the stories in order to inflame anti-Catholic feelings within the Restoration court and gain notoriety with the powerful men of the realm. He has been described as a 'liar and a scoundrel employed and motivated entirely by himself, drawing upon knowledge gained during a failed career.[31]

Oates is a complex character, the son of a minister, who, like many during the Commonwealth, changed his denomination from Anglican to Baptist before returning to the Church of England with the return of the monarchy in 1660. He studied at Cambridge, although, he was no model student and both Gonville and St Johns Colleges expelled him for his lack of academic ability. Minus a degree, Oates followed in the family vocation and became ordained into the Church of England in 1670. The first of many sexual scandals involving Oates took place during this period, resulting in him being charged with perjury after accusing a local school master of sodomy. His punishment was incarceration, but he escaped gaol and fled to London.

One of the few options open to a disgraced clergyman in the seventeenth century was to become a ship's chaplain in the Royal Navy. Scandal reappeared and Oates himself was accused of sodomy on board the ship the *Adventurer* to which he was assigned. At the time, acts of sodomy and homosexuality were capital crimes and he was only spared the noose as he was an ordained member of clergy.

His swift departure from the navy saw him take a very strange appointment, especially considering that he would go on and concoct the Popish Plot. Oates became an Anglican chaplain within the Catholic household of the 7th Duke of Norfolk, Henry Howard. By Ash Wednesday of 1677, after only being within the duke's household a few weeks, Oates had been converted to Roman Catholicism. What was even stranger was that not long after his road to Damascus conversion, Oates agreed to help write anti-Catholic literature with a Baptist rogue by the name of Israel Tonge.

Oates' acquaintance with Tonge was temporarily put on hold when he enrolled in the Royal English College situated in Valladolid, Spain under the tutorship of Jesuits, but just like his time at Cambridge, by summer 1678 he had been expelled from the Jesuit college as well. Within two months of his expulsion from the Royal English College he had returned to London and the anti-Catholic Tonge.

John Evelyn summarizes Titus Oates and articulates the confusion surrounding this rouge from a seventeenth century perspective.

> One thing my Lord said as to Oates, which I confess did exceedingly affect me: That a person who during his dispositions should so vauntingly brag that though he went over to the Church of Rome, yet he was never a papist, nor of their religion … but only as a spy; though he confessed he took their sacrament, worshipped images, went through their oaths …. but with the intent to come over again and betray them; that such a hypocrite.[32]

After returning from Spain, Oates and Tonge concocted a plot which claimed that the Jesuits were using leading Catholics within the court to help them to assassinate King Charles and convert England and Scotland back to the mother church of Rome. According to the pair, the alleged Jesuit plotters were going to achieve this deadly plan by sending Jesuits disguised as Presbyterian ministers to Scotland, who in turn would then start a rebellion. This would act as a signal to the Catholics at the royal court to assassinate the king so that the Duke of York could take the throne. The Jesuits would then burn London properly, unlike their attempt four years previously; the Great Fire of London in 1666. The Jesuits' failed attempt at burning down London was one of Oates' favourite topics of conversation. The outline of this fanatical plot by Tonge and Oates was self-published in a pamphlet.

On the morning of 13 August, Charles was on his way from the vast complex of Whitehall to take his daily constitutional walk within the royal park of St James. This was an activity that Charles often did by himself, or with the company of his beloved pet spaniels. While on his way to the royal park, an early scientist, Christopher Kirkby, who had previously demonstrated chemistry experiments for the king, approached His Majesty and told him of the alleged Popish Plot and the potential danger to his royal person. Charles agreed he would grant Kirkby an audience to explain what more he knew of this possible threat, then took his leave of the scientist and continued with his daily amble.

During the private audience with Charles, Kirkby introduced the king to Israel Tonge, who during the audience presented his majesty with a false dossier, outlining the details of the so-called plot. The result of this meeting was that Charles handed the document and information to one of his Privy councillors, Thomas Osborne, Earl of Danby, and requested that he investigate the plot to see if there was any truth in the tale. In order to strengthen their allegations, Oates and Tonge arranged an audience with Sir Edmund Berry Godfrey, a prominent and respected magistrate, who took down the pair's sworn depositions of the plot.

Charles became disgruntled with the affair and called both Tonge and Oates in front of his Privy Council on 27 and 28 September in the hope that his councillors would denounce their fabricated tale. Leaving his councillors to the task in hand, Charles decided to head to Newmarket for a day at the races instead of hearing Oates and Tonge. However, this would backfire on Charles spectacularly as the pair were buoyed up and confident after giving their dispositions to Sir Edmund Berry Godfrey. Their egos were further expanded by having a captive audience of some of the most powerful men of the realm to narrate their fantasy to.

Charles was therefore surprised and disappointed that he was called back from the racecourse by his Privy Council, who believed there were substantial reasons to fear Oates and Tonge's yarn. It is worth noting that some of His Majesty's Privy Councillors may have seen potential in using this false anti-Catholic 'plot', as well as the unsuspecting Oates and Tonge, for their own political advantage and profit, rather than actually believing that there was any real risk to their king and country. The list of persons accused by Oates is a like a roll call of prominent Catholic courtiers serving within Charles' civil service and government:

Catherine of Braganza (Queen Consort); Lord Arundell (Lord Chancellor, who also signed the Secret Treaty of Dover); Earl of Powis (Lord Treasurer); Sir William Godolphin (Lord Privy Seal); Viscount Stafford (Secretary of State); Edward Coleman (Secretary of State to the Duchess of York); Lord Belasyse (Captain General); Lord Petre (Lieutenant General); Sir Francis Ratcliffe (Major General); Sir George Wakeman (Surgeon General to the Queen's Household); Richard Langhorn (Advocate General).

What is strange is that although the list includes some of the most influential and prominent Catholics within the court and government, there is one notable absentee from that catalogue of names; Oates' former employer the Duke of Norfolk, Henry Howard, within whose household Oates had converted to Rome. Is it possible that Norfolk knew too much about Oates and was too dangerous to antagonise?

From the list, there was one Catholic courtier who would be found to be plotting, Edward Coleman, the personal secretary to the Duke of York's wife, Mary of Modena. Coleman had been writing to the French king's Catholic chaplain during 1675-76, asking for assistance to help reconvert England to Rome. For a conspirator, he was an amateur and naively kept copies of his correspondence. The letters were enough to convict Coleman of treason. Oates and his cronies had struck lucky and this gave credibility to their lies. Unfortunately for Coleman, he was hanged, drawn and quartered as a traitor.

The next stroke of luck to help give credit to Oates' fabrication was that the magistrate to whom Oates and Tonge had given their depositions went missing on 12 October. Five days later, on 17 October, Justice Berry Godfrey was discovered face down, dead in a ditch on Primrose Hill, London. There were clear marks around his neck, indicating that he had been strangled. However, in a true restoration theatrical twist, someone had also used his own sword and stabbed him, ramming the weapon hard into his heart with such force and violence that the blade went through his body; a literal demonstration of the word overkill. His clothes and valuables were also still on his person when he was discovered, his killer was therefore saying to those investigating the Popish Plot that Godfrey's murder was not a tragic mugging gone wrong, but that his murder was to be unmistakably linked to Oates fantasy plot. The truth behind Sir Edmund Berry Godfrey's death remains unresolved to this day.

Some claimed that the additional theatrical sword through his heart was an attempt to cover up that he had committed suicide by hanging. However, the coroner would rule that his death was due to murder. This would be enough to provoke the exasperated London mob into overdrive and assume that Godfrey had been murdered by Papists embroiled in the plot, in order to stop him from investigating the alleged political scandal. It is also dubious that Justice Berry Godfrey and Edward Coleman were known to be acquainted. So the fact that one was arrested as the result of Oates' allegations and then within a week the other had been killed, it reeks of political plot, scandal and collusion. All this certainly hints at there being foul play by someone who wanted to encourage and strengthen Oates' fabrication.

Another factor that helped give credence to Oates and Tonge's web of lies was the dire economic climate at the time the plot was brought to the public's attention, not to mention a high level of unemployment. With many disenchanted men with nothing to do but think about their ill fortunes, the plot gave them something to blame their situation on, which would not have helped the suspicious anti-Catholic climate.

The tragic fallout from Oates' web of lies meant that thirty-five innocent Catholics, many of whom were clergy, were prosecuted and executed as traitors, on the back of the alleged plot. These trials and the subsequent punishment were encouraged by the London mob. Within the Catholic church it was the Jesuits who suffered the worst persecution as a fallout from the investigation. In the north, away from the influence of London and the gossip, in places such as Lincolnshire, Derbyshire and Durham, Catholics and Jesuits were less persecuted and often left alone.

One of the victims in London of the fabricated plot was Colonel Richard Talbot. Ironically, Talbot was apprehended on 5 November 1678, the anniversary of the failed Gunpowder Plot.

> Where there has been further information given us upon touching a rebellion ... whereby it appears that Richard Talbolt was general ... and that they had received and accepted their several commissions from the Pope as by affidavit made by Titus Oates .... we therefore authorize and require you forthwith ... to be immediately apprehended and kept safe in custody until further notice.[33]

The Popish Plot aided the growing number of Exclusionists to gain support in the House of Commons, by riding on the general anti-Catholic feeling and suspicion of what would happen if York were to inherit the throne. As a result, the MPs voted overwhelmingly to exclude James from the throne. However after both votes, Charles would use his royal prerogative to promptly dissolve the parliaments to stop the motions carrying any further and becoming law.

The highest status victim of Oates' vicious web of lies was William Howard, 1st Viscount Stafford, a Catholic peer with a history of loyalty to the monarchy throughout the Civil Wars, Charles' exile and after the Restoration. Religious persecution seems to have run in his family as his grandfather, Philip Howard, the 20th Earl of Arundel, was also held in the Tower of London for his Catholicism in 1585 by Elizabeth I, as he was considered a danger after the fall of Mary Queen of Scots. He would not be freed because fear of Catholicism intensified after the failed invasion of the Spanish Armada. Arundel died in the Tower, after ten years of incarceration.

Under Charles I, Howard had been created the 1st Viscount Stafford in November 1640. With the start of the bloody Civil Wars, the Staffords relocated to Antwerp. They lost their English property and assets due to the Viscount's refusal to attend the Anglican Communion and his loyalty to the crown during the Civil Wars and the Commonwealth. After the fall of Charles I and his execution, Stafford would assist the exiled court by carrying out diplomatic errands to the Low Countries, Rome, and the Palatine. With a history like this, it is hard to comprehend why his peers would think that he was capable of treason thirty years later. With the restoration of the crown, came the restoration of the family estate and lands to Stafford. As a Catholic, life under Charles II, certainly at the beginning of his reign, was reason enough for the Staffords to live a private and quiet life, without religious persecution in their restored family home. He had surely earned his retirement after his loyal service.

Viscount Stafford's only involvement within the Restoration's politics was to support both the king and the Duke of York in attempting to revoke anti-Catholic legislation, such as the Test Act in 1672. This act of political conscience may well in itself have brought him to the attention of the conspirators, thus making himself a target of their plot.

Stafford's name was linked with Oates' plethora of lies from the plot's exposure, primarily as he was a well-known Catholic peer. In 1678, Stafford went from being rumoured of being involved, to being a full suspect, when the king was finally convinced of the Viscount's possible involvement with the plot. This change came about due to a new witness materialising called Stephen Dugdale, whose only difference from Oates was his 'neat appearance and educated manner.'[34]

It is interesting to note that in Dugdale's version of the Popish Plot, it was both Charles and the Duke of Monmouth who were the intended targets to be assassinated by the Jesuits. The reasoning for Monmouth to also be eliminated along with the king was to prevent an Anglican succession of the throne. The flaw to this thinking by the plotters is that they had forgotten about a legitimate Protestant candidate, William of Orange and his wife Mary, who had equal if not better rights to the throne than their cousin Monmouth.

Evidence from a more respectable witness meant that Stafford and four other Catholic peers, Lord Arundell, Lord Belasyse, Lord Petre and the Earl of Powis were arrested and taken to the Tower on 31 October 1678. However, although the Lords, especially Stafford, ended up in the Tower, there was still doubt in Charles' mind as to their implication and guilt. This doubt is shown when he did two very telling things. Firstly, Charles dissolved parliament in order for more investigations into the plot to be carried out, but more accurately into the five Lords, including Stafford's alleged involvement. Secondly, Charles was prepared to offer Stafford a full royal pardon if he pleaded guilty, thus hopefully bringing the plot and scandal to an end, and avoid the execution of a loyal lord. Stafford was unprepared to confess to something he did not do and politely refused the king's offer, instead requesting he be tried by a court of his peers.

Almost thirteen months after he had been committed to the Tower on charges of High Treason, Lord Stafford was the first of the Catholic lords to stand trial. The legal proceedings started on 29 November 1679 in the House of Lords. During his trial, Titus Oates and Stephen Dugdale gave evidence to Stafford's peers and colleagues. Unfortunately for Stafford, he was put on trial before the change to the law in 1695, which meant he was not entitled to counsel to help defend him. The aged lord therefore had to defend himself and whether it was his age, the effect of being incarcerated in the Tower, fear, or a mixture of all three, Stafford struggled to defend himself against Oates and his cronies.

Among the peers that went on to convict him and thus send an innocent man to a cruel death, were members of his own family. Some of Howard's family held grudges over old feuds and seven out of eight of them found their kinsman guilty. The vote, held on 7 December 1680, convicted Stafford by fifty-five votes to thirty-one. On this day, John Evelyn said the following on the result of the trial:

> It was observed that all his family condemned him, except his nephew, the Lord of Arundel's son, the Duke of Norfolk.... God only searches hearts, can discover the truth. Lord Stafford was not a man beloved, especially of his own family.[35]

William Howard, 1st Viscount Stafford would not live to see the new year and was executed by beheading, as privilege of being a peer of the realm, thus escaping the more gruesome hanging, drawing and quartering; he was duly executed upon Tower Hill, on 29 December 1680. The events of the Popish Plot meant that the Anglican Protestants migrated towards the Protestant Duke of Monmouth and he became more embroiled in their plans as an alternative heir to the English, Scottish and Irish throne. The plot would also tighten the distrust in relations between James Duke of York and his nephew James Duke of Monmouth. It was was, therefore, the spark that would light the fuse and eventually lead Monmouth into rebellion and his downfall.

Chapter 9

Monmouth and the Exclusion Crisis

The Exclusion Crisis is the name given to the political storm that surrounded the controversial idea of excluding James Duke of York from the throne due to his Catholic faith. During the seventeenth century, religion and politics went together hand in hand, both within the houses of parliament, as well as at the royal court.

James was the heir to the throne as Charles and Catherine had failed to have children to inherit. Unlike Henry VIII, who faced a similar crisis during his reign, Charles (surprisingly for a man who had a notorious passion for women), refused to trade his wife for a younger model to order to attempt to achieve this goal, despite the Earl of Shaftesbury, who bravely risked the king's wrath by suggesting this as an alternative to the policy of Exclusion. The crisis spanned the last three parliaments of Charles II's reign and ended with the dissolution of the Oxford Parliament during the spring of 1681. Frustrated and at a loss as to what else to do to pacify the Exclusionists without giving them what they wanted, Charles dismissed his Parliament in the last absolutist directive of any monarch in British history.

With the help of hindsight, some historians have questioned if the word 'crisis' was in fact an accurate description for the last three parliaments. It is, however, too simplistic to say that this is an exaggeration, because at the time Charles, his government ministers and the many who had lived through the turbulent times of the Civil Wars, felt that there was a genuine threat to the peace. However, what they felt at the time does not reflect the reality of the parliamentary sessions. You could be forgiven for thinking that parliament did not have any other matters of business to deal with during this period. This of course was not the case. Shaftesbury and the Exclusionists were just particularly good at keeping the issue of Exclusion at the top of the political agenda. Charles felt that there was a threat to the monarchy if he allowed parliament to dictate the succession of the crown, while the early Whigs feared that if a Catholic monarch was allowed to take the throne, it would threaten British liberty and laws. Both sides were angry at the past and fearful of the future and as a result, this clouded their judgment for the present.

These fears had been inflamed through recent circumstances, namely the discovery of the so-called Popish Plot, which had caused suspicion to fall on many leading Catholic MPs and Lords, and had even resulted in several high profile convictions. The thought of the Duke of York taking the throne was now feared even more than before, and was heightened further when Charles became dangerously ill during the summer of 1679. For ten days at the end of the summer, the prospect of a Catholic monarch became a very real prospect.

The first Exclusion Bill was introduced to the House of Commons on 11 May 1679 by William, Lord Russell. Ten days later, on 21 May, the bill had passed both its first and second reading in the House. The only way Charles could halt the bill from progressing any further and reaching the House of Lords was to prorogue the parliamentary session on 27 May, before finally dissolving parliament six weeks later on 3 July. However, this was not going to stop Russell or Shaftesbury in their goal of Exclusion; for them this was just a temporary blip.

The Exclusionists were able to organize themselves and hone their support during the period between the parliamentary sessions. Parliament was meant to have reconvened in October 1679, but Charles prorogued Parliament again, giving the Exclusionists until October 1680 to recruit more MPs to their cause.

The second Exclusion Parliament started on 21 October 1680, fifteen months after the last session was abruptly stopped. On 15 November, Shaftesbury introduced the Exclusion Bill to the House of Lords with an impassioned speech, but was challenged by George Savile, Lord Halifax. The exchange was witnessed by two key people, the first being the Duke of Monmouth but the second was more important; it was the king himself. In the run up to the debate in the upper house, Charles, with the help of Halifax, had canvassed and petitioned the members of the Lords, seeking support for the Duke of York and for the defeat of the Exclusion Bill. The canvassing and debate had worked and the bill was defeated in the House of Lords by sixty-three to thirty. Charles had defeated the Exclusionists without having to dissolve Parliament.

Unsurprisingly, one of the members of the House of Lords who voted in favour of Exclusion was Monmouth himself. The justification Monmouth gave for voting for the bill was that he feared his uncle, the Duke of York, was acting maliciously against the king; an expression which Charles was said to have described as 'the kiss of Judas'.[36]

In the aftermath of the defeated Exclusion Bill, Monmouth was still attracting attention within court, much to the annoyance of some. In a letter to the Duke of Ormond, the Earl of Ossory wrote:

> All the world now visits the Duke of Monmouth; but considering how affairs are between the King and him, I think it not respectful in me towards his Majesty to make that complaint.[37]

The Exclusionists' next tactic was to debate how to restrict any royal powers of any Catholic, but specifically the Duke of York, should they inherit the throne. Another personal angle that the Lords debated was whether Charles should remarry. The Lords had gone too far and Charles prorogued Parliament again before finally dissolving both houses on 18 January 1681.

The next parliament would be the Oxford Parliament, when Charles would end the political avenue of Exclusion once and for all. After the close of the Oxford Parliament there were a hardcore number of Exclusionists, who were frustrated by their lack of success. Indeed, they were so disheartened that they were happy to risk their lives to attempt to achieve their political goal through less than democratic methods.

These foolhardy men would become entangled in such folly as the foiled Rye House Plot (1683). There were men who managed to escape retribution for their role within that plot, such as Archibald Campbell, the 9th Earl of Argyll, who would go on to help Monmouth in his rebellion in 1685. The Exclusionists were men ahead of their political time. Their ideas became reality in 1688 when William and Mary took the throne on the proviso that they were constitutional monarchs; a political system still in place in the twenty-first century.

Although the Exclusionists disliked the idea of York inheriting the throne of England, Ireland and Scotland, he did have something that Monmouth did not have; York was the legitimate son of a monarch and his queen. In reality, despite Monmouth's popularity with the populace and his close resemblance to his father, both in looks as well as his Protestant faith, the crux of the matter was that Monmouth was illegitimate. The Exclusionist, Robert Fergusson, printed a pamphlet saying that during his exile, Charles had married Monmouth's mother, Lucy Walter. The king was always firm in his response regarding this matter, always categorically denying that he ever married her. This brings up the question of who, if the dukes of Monmouth and York were not suitable to sit on the throne, was in fact a better alternative candidate to inherit the British throne?

The most logical choice was the Duke of York's son-in-law and nephew, Prince William of Orange, who also held the title of Stadtholder of Holland, Zeeland, Utrecht, Gelderland and Overijssel. William's mother was the eldest daughter of Charles I; thus making her the sister of both the king and the Duke of York. William's connection to the English throne through his mother meant that he was fourth in line to the throne in his own right. His claim was further strengthened when he married his first cousin, Princess Mary, who as the Duke of York's eldest child, was next in line to the throne after her father. Therefore, William's claim to the succession was doubly stronger than the Exclusionists' claim for the Duke of Monmouth.

William was also Protestant, which was another reason why he was a better alternative heir to the throne compared to his uncle James. At this time, the north of Europe was predominately Protestant, in William's case, Calvinist. Calvinism emerged during the post-Reformation period in Geneva, and the movement was named after its founder, John Calvin. It would become another reformed alternative to Roman Catholicism. The Calvinists disagreed with some elements of the reformed doctrine followed by the Lutherans, most notably the use of church hierarchy and their belief in predestination. After the Glorious Revolution of 1688, when William took the British throne, he diplomatically converted to the Anglican communion.

The biggest problem that made William a less attractive alternative to the throne with the general public was his foreignness. Although, Monmouth was born in Rotterdam, while Charles II was in exile, he was by all accounts perceived as being English rather than foreign, in dress, behaviour, speech and looks. William on the other hand spoke with a heavy Dutch accent, as well as having the mannerisms of a foreigner.

One of the main reasons that the Duke of Monmouth may have been more appealing to the parliamentary establishment might, ironically, have actually been his illegitimacy. By making him the heir this would automatically transform the monarchy. Shifting the succession to the Duke of Monmouth would provide an ideal opportunity for the introduction of various constitutional reforms on how the nation was ruled. By doing so, this would fulfill what the Commonwealth under Cromwell had hoped to do, but had ultimately failed to accomplish. By allowing an illegitimate son to inherit the throne, parliament would hopefully be able to establish a more limited form of monarchy.

With hindsight, we know that William and his wife Mary were invited to take the throne by the British establishment to become their chosen monarch. William and Mary's joint reign would be the first in our history that saw the role of the monarchy step back and become a figurehead rather than ruler; allowing a democratically elected parliament to rule the nation. Even though the use of the term 'democratically elected' in the seventeenth and eighteenth century is nowhere near to what we would consider it to be today, this still marked the beginning of a new chapter in the history of British politics.

Chapter 10

The Road to Treason

In February 1679, a general election for the House of Commons was called, and once again the Duke of York's Catholic faith was becoming politically awkward for his brother, Charles. All the king wanted to do was to protect his brother and retain him as his only heir. However, the newly elected Parliament was made up of a large majority of MPs who were affiliated with the Country political faction. These men were predominately Anglican, pro-parliament, anti-Catholic and sought a monarch who would work with the elected Houses of Parliament, rather than control them. For them the thought of a Catholic heir meant autocratic rule.

As a consequence of the election result, Charles asked his brother to reconsider his faith, but like many converts to any faith, York was zealous and refused to let the whim of parliament dictate the fate of his immortal soul. In order to keep him politically safe, Charles was left with no alternative but to send his brother into exile. Charles also hoped that with York's absence, the growing political unrest would not develop into a new civil crisis and revolt. Thus York, accompanied by his wife and family, would reluctantly leave Whitehall and the royal court for Europe, heading for Brussels with no idea when he would be allowed to return to Britain and his inheritance.

When Charles became ill in late August 1679, the Exclusionist cause would accelerate and bring about the political crisis that would be paramount to the Duke of Monmouth's fate. Before his illness, Charles had spent a relaxing summer at Windsor, fishing on the Thames, at Datchet, sometimes accompanied by one of his favourite mistresses, Nell Gwyn, who had a house close to the castle (her former home is now a Chinese restaurant that still bears her name). With Parliament dissolved and the Privy Council adjourned for the summer, Charles had very little to worry about apart from being a merry monarch.

The Duke of Monmouth was part of his father's court at the time Charles was taken ill. He was on hand throughout the king's illness as the Duke of York was still on the continent, in exile, oblivious to his brother's change in health. Until this time in his life, the forty-nine year old monarch had been in fine health and had a good level of fitness. He was known for his love of sport and regularly played Real Tennis, fenced and took daily constitutional walks with his beloved pet spaniels. Nothing seemed unusual when the king contracted a cold upon returning from a trip sailing on the south coast. On 23 August, his cold became more serious when his temperature rose to a high fever. Over the next few days, the fever rose and fell as he developed more worrying symptoms, such as excessive sweating and vomiting, accompanied by a severe thirst in conjunction with an inability to pass water. The doctors who were called to treat the king used the traditional seventeenth-century cure all of applying leeches, which was hoped would help alleviate the king's illness. Although the seventeenth century was at the dawn of scientific discovery, this had not filtered through to the medical profession at the time of Charles' illness.

The Duke of Monmouth was also, incidentally, the most senior courtier at Windsor when the king took ill and had the duty of communicating his father's illness to the Lord Mayor of London. The Earl of Sunderland, however, thought that Monmouth should also have communicated the potentially deadly situation to the Duke of York, as well as the Lord Mayor of London. Sunderland was so put out by Monmouth's thoughtlessness that he took it upon himself to write and inform the Duke of York of the king's illness. As soon as York received the letter on 28 August, he packed his bags and decided to return to court, without permission to leave his exile.

As Sunderland's letter was heading to Europe, the king's condition seemed to exacerbate and worsen even further when he developed seizures and lost the control of his bowels. It was bad enough that the poor king was so dangerously ill, but he was not even given peace and privacy in which to recuperate, having no less than seven quack doctors constantly present in his bedchamber regularly poking and prodding him. Also present in his bedchamber were half the Privy Council, who had come to court upon hearing of the king's illness as well as his usual gentlemen of the bedchamber and servants.

The illness was thankfully only short lived, lasting just over a week. By the time York had returned to court after three days of hard travel, over land and sea, presumably fearful of the fact that he may have lost his brother, apprehensive that he may be about to take the throne as a practising Catholic and worried about the political and social repercussion of leaving exile, he found the king, no longer dangerously ill, but dressed and waiting for his barber to groom him.

On 12 September, the day after the Duke of York arrived back from exile to find his brother both hale and hearty, Charles summoned Monmouth to his chamber. During their meeting, the king told him that he had to resign his post of Lord General and to go to the continent for a season. This must have come to Monmouth as both an insult and a shock after caring and worrying about his father's health the previous few weeks. At first, the duke refused to obey his father's request to leave court and country. In desperation, Monmouth called a meeting of his Exclusionist supporters, Shaftesbury chief among them, who in turn managed to persuade a disheartened and hurt Monmouth to obey the king's orders. Monmouth left London and arrived in the Dutch town of Utrecht on 24 September 1679.

It was probably during this first exile that Monmouth may have started to change how he thought about Exclusionist politics. This would have been because he now had time and selfish motivation to think about how Exclusion might benefit him. These thoughts would have been clouded by his angry, frustrated and resentful feelings towards both his father and uncle. The arguments and theories of Shaftesbury and his cronies were persuasive and offered a way to vent his frustrated feelings of abandonment. This exile marked the beginning of Monmouth's road to Tower Hill and his fall from grace.

It is worth remembering that there were two precedents within English history of royal bastards inheriting the throne. In 1544, Henry VIII, had declared that if Edward, his only son by Jane Seymour, were to die childless, then his daughters, Princesses Mary and Elizabeth, both of whom had been declared illegitimate through acts of parliament, would become eligible to succeed to the throne. Neither Elizabeth nor Mary had their illegitimate status removed before they started their reigns in 1553 and 1558 respectively. This may have provided the Duke of Monmouth with hope that he too could legally take the throne upon his father's death.

Not long into Monmouth's exile and subsequent arrival at the court of his cousins, William and Mary, a new general election was called in Britain, the results of which saw Shaftesbury's Exclusionists and Country faction take the majority of seats within the House of Commons. However, this session of Parliament was short lived; Charles had had enough of the Exclusion Crisis. The king didn't need his Parliament any longer as he had secured financial support from France through the Treaty of Dover. Therefore, Charles dissolved the parliament. Had this parliament lasted longer and Charles had no ready supply of funds, history as well as Monmouth's fate may have been rather different.

The result of this short-lived parliamentary session reflected the view of London at the time. Traditionally, November had always been a month with both political and religious meaning that encouraged anti-Catholic views. This is due to the anniversary of the discovery of the Gunpowder Plot, on 5 November 1605. It was also the month that the Protestant Queen Elizabeth I ascended the throne upon the death of her notorious Catholic sister, 'Bloody' Mary Tudor. In 1679, November was a good indicator of the anti-Catholic climate that Monmouth had left only a few weeks previously. Charles had to move the Protestant focus of the Exclusionists away from his son in order to avoid tensions boiling over into violence and possible rebellion.

In seventeenth-century London, the traditional burning of the 'Guy' was often depicted as the Pope instead of Guy Fawkes. The biggest celebration was held on 17 November to commemorate the date of Elizabeth I's ascension to the throne. The celebrations would start at 3 am when the bells of London rang out, followed by an anti-Catholic procession starting in east London from Moorgate, before finally ending at Temple Bar near St Paul's Cathedral. Those taking part in the 1679 procession carried images of the murdered Justice, Edmund Berry Godfrey, who was seen to be part of the Popish Plot, alongside the usual anti-Catholic depictions of Catholic clergy carrying bloody daggers, various orders of Catholic friars and a variety of images depicting Bishops, Cardinals and the Pope. Anti-Catholic songs were sung, many praising Queen Elizabeth, such as this example which was sung by a statue of the queen in Temple Bar:

> Cease, cease thou Norfolk Cardinal,
> See yonder stand Queen Bess,
> Who sav'd our souls from Popish thrall,
> Oh Queen Bess, Queen Bess, Queen Bess!
> Your Popish plot,
> And Smithfield threat,
> We do not fear at all,
> For lo! Beneath Queen Bess's feet,
> You fall, you fall, you fall.
> Now God Preserve Great Charles our King,
> And eke all honest men,
> And traitors all to justice bring:
> Amen, Amen, Amen.

Having too much time on his hands and isolated from his friends, Monmouth became fed up in his European exile and decided to return to London without permission. He arrived in the capital at the height of anti-Catholic fever on 27 November, much to the anger of the king. The city had been lit up by the light of hundreds of bonfires; the church bells of the city tolled at the news of the duke's return. All Charles could do was order his arrogant and sulky son back into exile. The duke was encouraged by his supporters and long suffering wife Anne to return to Europe, but stubbornly decided to ignore them and the wishes of his father. The consequence of this refusal to return to exile resulted in a deterioration of Monmouth's relationship with Charles.

In an impetus attempt to try and build bridges with the king and return to his life at court, Monmouth wrote to his father in May 1680, asking after his health. Charles, in an uncharacteristic gesture of harsh authoritativeness towards his son, asked the Earl of Godolphin to inform the duke that his obedience and return to exile would be the only way in which he would forgive him. The episode is referred to in a letter from one Col. Cooke to the Marquis of Ormond:

> How long the Duke of Monmouth have been in town I know not; but this I do that last Thursday he send… a letter to the King both to acquaint His Majesty that he was returned and to beseech His Majesty's permission to kiss his hand. The King in a great fury returned this answer commanded that he immediately begone again, positively refusing to see him… The Duke urged his innocence and desired to come to his trial, that banishment was the proper badge of a malefactor…some arraign his grace with double guilt disloyalty and undutifulness, both to King and parent. Others do not only pity him…he is certainly at present the idol of the people.[38]

It seems Charles had finally given up forgiving his first born son. A month after telling Monmouth to return to Europe via the Earl of Godolphin, Charles re-issued a declaration reiterating that he had only been married once and that to the current queen, Catherine of Braganza. This was in an effort to quash the Exclusionist fantasy that he had been married during the dark days of the Commonwealth to Monmouth's mother, Lucy Walter.

Whether through mutual politics or that Monmouth now found himself without the guidance of his father, it was at this time that Monmouth and the Earl of Shaftesbury became closer. This may have been the point when treason was disguised as political evolution and Monmouth became its popular figure head.

In the summer of 1680, the Duke of Monmouth set out on a progress around Chichester and then the south-west of England. Royal progresses had previously been the only way that medieval monarchs could be seen by their subjects. Among their engagements, the medieval monarchs would perform a ritual known as 'Touching of the King's Evil', a practice that was was popular in both France and England and was said to have been started in the eleventh century. In the ritual, the monarch would touch people who had Scrofula, more commonly known as the 'King's Evil', and 'cure' them. The disease itself involved the swelling of the lymph nodes and is now thought to have probably been tuberculosis. As well as performing the ritual, the king or queen would also attend local assizes and court circuits. On his first progress, the Duke of Monmouth made contact and visited with the nobility within Cheshire and the south-west of England. This was to gauge the level of support that there was for the Whigs and their Exclusion policy, loosely disguised as a summer of social gatherings among the great and the good of the land. While he travelled around with an entourage of courtiers and hangers on, the local peasants would come out and greet him, becoming excited as they glimpsed the glamorous, handsome and heroic duke who had the reputation of being a brave military hero.

The Exclusionist progress started within a territory that was primed with pro-Exclusion feeling. In the famously anti-Catholic, Sussex town of Chichester, it is said that the locals spat at the sound of York's name. Monmouth's progress was recorded in the following lines taken from John Dryden's, satirical poem; *Absalom and Achitophel*:

> Impatient of high hopes, urg'd with renown,
> And fir'd with near possession of a crown,
> Th' admiring crowd are dazzled with surprise,
> And on his goodly person feed their eyes.
> His joy conceal'd, he sets himself to show.

The next destination on Monmouth's progress was the stately home of Longleat House, owned by Thomas Thynne. While the duke was traveling towards the Longleat estate, all the small village and town lanes he passed through were full of local country people come to cheer and wave him on his way; Monmouth was undertaking a royal progress in all but name.

After his stay at Longleat House, Monmouth continued progressing through the West Country, paying a call on Sir John Sydenham at Brimpton House, Sir William Strode of Barrington Court, Edmund Prideaux at Ford Abbey, and George Speke at White Lodge in Hinton Park.

While the Duke was at Hinton Park, a peasant woman by the name of Elizabeth Parcet, touched his hand. She hoped that Monmouth was royal enough to enable the ritual of Touching the King's Evil to happen. Two days after she had touched Monmouth, all of her wounds started to heal.

> She prest in amongst a crowd of people and caught him by the hand, his glove being on… she not being herewith satisfied with this first attempt of touching his glove only, but her mind was she must touch part of his bare skin.[39]

Monmouth and his Exclusionist supporters could not have hoped for something so serendipitous to have happened while he was away on his progress. This gave the Exclusionists the perfect evidence to prove that Monmouth should be the legitimate heir to the throne; it was, in short, seventeenth century PR gold dust. The practice of Touching the King's Evil had actually fallen out of favour under Charles I, but upon the Restoration, his son, Charles II, had resurrected the ritual as a way of interacting with his people. Charles would hold these ceremonies at Whitehall and touch hundreds of people at one time. Each of the patients would also be given a gold coin known as a 'Touchpiece'. It is thought that Charles II touched 92,107 sick people within his twenty-five year reign. The practice would in fact die out with the Stuart dynasty, with the last English monarch to practice it being Queen Anne.

From White Lodge, Monmouth and his followers travelled into the southern county of Devon, to the town of Cloyton, just seven miles from Lyme Regis where in 1685, he would land and launch his rebellion. From Cloyton, the duke went on to Otterton House, and then to Exeter, where he was met by a great crowd of 20,000 local people. From there, he went back to White Lackington House, before staying at Clifton House. He would then start his return to London, calling in again at the Longleat estate.

What made the Duke of Monmouth popular with the people of the West Country was that he didn't just sit on his horse and wave at the crowds of people. Instead, he made contact with them the way the modern royals do when they stop to interact with the crowds at public engagements. Some of the more fun and hands on activities that Monmouth engaged in included wrestling with locals and jumping on to their horses. In return for his participation, the people he met happily taught him their traditional country dances in return for him showing them some courtly dance steps. He indulged in their way of life, joining them at picnics and eating their humble everyday food and drink, including ciders and elderberry wine.

Monmouth was, to use the modern parlance, a man of the people. The duke clearly had the same charisma of modern day celebrity. As well as being of the Protestant faith, he also had an infectious charm, striking good looks inherited from his father, and a proven reputation of being a brave and successful military hero. Together, these traits made him an attractive and safe alternative heir to the throne.

The Oxford parliamentary session of 1681 is historic in the fact it was the last time that an English monarch was able to dissolve parliament at their own will and rule instead as an absolute monarch. This parliamentary session was the fifth and last of the reign of Charles II. It is important to the fate of the Duke of Monmouth as it would effectively put an end to the legal route of Exclusion, meaning those who wanted to disinherit the future James II from the throne had no option but to pursue treasonous routes to achieve their objective.

The King had decided to hold his last parliamentary session away from the pro-Exclusion, anti-Catholic palace of Westminster in order to avoid riots within the city, as well as violence directed at his court. He chose the city of Oxford as it had a proven history of being loyal towards the monarchy. The parliamentary session started on 21 March 1681 and lasted a little more than a week before Charles dissolved it and released his MPs for the very last time. However, this historic session of government was closed with one of the king's most eloquent speeches of his reign:

> It is much my interest and it shall be as much my Care as Yours, to preserve the Liberty of the Subjects; because the Crown can never be safe when that is in danger: And I wou'd have you likewise be convinc'd, that neither your Liberties and Properties can subsist long, when the just Rights and Prerogatives of the Crown are invaded or the Honour of the Government brought low, and into Disreputation.[40]

After referring to why the stability of the nation was important for both crown and government alike, Charles went on to say how he did not dislike his parliament. This was despite his actions, which were taken in frustration, and his repeated postponements of their debates and deliberations. The speech was Charles' attempt to demonstrate to parliament and for the prosperity of history that he was not like his father in his relationship with his parliament.

> I let you see by my calling Parliament shall make me out of love with them; and by Means; offer you another Opportunity of providing for our Security here by giving that Countenance and Protection to our Neighbours and Allies, which you can not but expect from Us.[41]

Charles went on to reiterate his position on the succession of his throne, before bringing the Oxford Parliament to a close by saying:

> What I have formerly, and often declared touching the succession I cannot depart from. But to remove all reasonable Fears that may arise from the Possibility of a Popish Successor's coming to the Crown; if means can be found, that in such a Case the Administration of the Government may remain in Protestant Hands I shall be ready to hearken to any such expedient by which religion might be preserv'd and Monarch not destroy'd. I must therefore earnestly recommend to you to provide for the religion and government together with regard to one another because they support each other....I conclude with this advice to You, the rules and measures of all your Votes may be the known and establish'd Laws of the land which neither can nor ought to be departed from nor changed but by act of Parliament: and I reasonably require, That you make the Laws your Rule because I am Resolv'd they shall be mine.[42]

Charles therefore had the last say on the issue of Exclusion. With the Exclusionist and Country faction defeated in Oxford, the Court faction went on to regain control of London through the election of a pro-Court Sheriff in July 1682. Soon afterwards, Shaftesbury left England for a self-imposed exile and died in Amsterdam, in early 1683. With no strong leadership left and all the legal and political avenues to achieve Exclusion concluded; treason was now the only avenue open for the Exclusionists.

During the late summer of 1682, the Duke of Monmouth undertook a second progress, travelling through the counties of Lancashire,

Staffordshire, Worcestershire and Cheshire. Compared to his first progress, this one caused both the king and Duke of York enormous alarm as it did not come to pass without embarrassment or disturbance. Just like the first progress, its purpose was for Monmouth to help the Exclusionists establish the magnitude of support for their cause and to gauge the people's feelings towards him becoming the possible Protestant heir to his father's throne. One of the men whom the duke visited while in the north-east was Charles Gerard, Earl of Macclesfield.

The Duke of Monmouth paid a visit to the county of Staffordshire before heading to neighbouring Cheshire. In Cheshire, Monmouth processed into the old Roman settlement of Chester with his entourage, thought to have been made up of between 120 and 200 men on horseback. This extravagant and theatrical entrance encouraged thousands of onlookers to come and watch, all eager to catch a look at the king's son, the Duke of Monmouth. This would have been many people's only chance to witness some of the splendour and opulence of the Restoration court away from London. Monmouth was greeted by the mayor and local dignitaries, who treated him as if he was the king. During his visit he enjoyed attending the races, where he won a fortune in plate and money, and the people showed their affection towards him by lighting bonfires in his honour.

Not everyone in Cheshire was happy to hear of the arrival of the duke. Monmouth would face opposition to the progress and the Exclusionist cause from the local Tory supporters, who tried to put the bonfires out in sign of protest. The local peasants, who were possibly uninterested in the politics behind the quenching of the bonfires, merely saw this as an act by people wishing to ruin their celebrations and fun. As a consequence, local rioting started.

In the days that followed the rioting in Cheshire, the Duke of Monmouth moved around the north; heading to Dunham, Stoaken Heath, Warrington, Trentham Hall, Newcastle and Stafford. During his tour between Wallasey and Liverpool, Monmouth saw an opportunity to help 'cure' a child by performing the ritual of the 'King's Evil'. Once again, Monmouth had undertaken an act exclusively reserved for the reigning monarch to perform. By doing this once he had taken a politically risky liberty, by doing it again on a second discouraged progress, it became clear that Charles would not forgive his errant son, who was publicly and deliberately antagonising both the local Tories and his father. On 20 September, while he was dining in Stafford, a warrant for his arrest was presented to Monmouth from the Secretary of State. The crime of which the duke had been accused was inciting riots in Chester and his arrest obviously immediately put an end to his second progress. It was the mayor who delicately broke the news to Monmouth that he was about to be taken into custody, although he diplomatically stated out loud that he abhorred traitorous activity. The duke remained calm and asked the mayor to propose a toast to his father, the king, before leaving with them.

Under arrest, Monmouth was escorted back towards London. On the way, the party travelled through the Midland city of Coventry, where several hundred people came out to cheer him, despite being under arrest. On the sixth day after his arrest, the escort reached St Albans in Hertfordshire, where they were met by Thomas Armstrong who had ridden to London ahead of the party and secured the duke a habeas corpus, meaning that Monmouth needed to be brought in front of a court of law so that all charges against him needed to be stated and substantiated. The party moved swiftly to London, where a reluctant Monmouth was brought to Whitehall under the pretence that his father wanted to speak to him. Frustrated and angry, Monmouth refused to co-operate when he discovered that the king did not want to see him. Indeed, he became so frustrated with the proceedings that he was re-arrested for walking out of the hearing. This new incident resulted in him being put under house arrest. Eventually, the Duke was released a few days later, after a sizeable bail payment had been made.

While in custody in John Ramsey's home, Monmouth received visits from his Whig supporters, including Russell and Shaftesbury. However, not long after Monmouth's capture, Shaftesbury decided that he had become more of a liability than a political advantage. Ever the political survivor, Shaftesbury decided that it was time to disassociate himself from Monmouth.

Chapter 11

The Rye House Plot

In the months leading up to his exile and subsequent death, Shaftesbury was arrested on trumped up charges of treason and incarcerated in the Tower to await trial. The given reason was that he had planned a war against the king at Oxford, the evidence against him being a Bill of Association. With the Oxford Parliament dissolved, the king finally felt confident to be able to have Shaftesbury arrested. The Earl was fortunate and managed to escape his charges when a jury made up of a majority of Whigs sympathizers ruled that the bills of indictment had no case to answer. It was during his time held in the Tower that the satirical poet of the day, John Dryden, published his scandalous political work, *Absalom and Architophel*, in which, as previously noted, Shaftesbury did not come across particularly well.

In September 1682, after his release from the Tower, Shaftesbury retired to his home, Thanet House on Aldergate Street in London. He had received medical care whilst in the Tower from the king's own doctor and he must have felt that he was nearing the end of his life. Monmouth and William, Lord Russell, visited their old comrade while he was sick. During this visit, Shaftesbury, clearly frustrated that he was running out of time and had failed to achieve his political goals, expressed his desire to start a rebellion by seizing the king's guards and storming London. Both Monmouth and Russell were taken by surprise at Shaftesbury's uncharacteristicly feverish and hot-headed scheme. Russell recalled how Monmouth 'took me by the hand and told me kindly: my Lord I see you and I are of a temper; did you ever hear so horrid a thing?'[43]

Although Monmouth and Russell were unconvinced by Shaftesbury's plans, the Earl was eager to continue plotting and planning. In hopes of avoiding arrest, during the dead of night he moved from Thanet House to the east London dock area of Wapping. For the next few weeks, he planned and schemed with extreme Whigs such as the disgruntled Scot, Robert Ferguson. Shaftesbury arranged a meeting of like-minded men in mid-November. It is said that Russell and Monmouth arrived together and were joined later by Lord Grey and Thomas Armstrong, but they found that Shaftesbury was not coming in person.

Soon after, the Earl of Shaftesbury received information that confirmed Monmouth and Russell's reluctance; there were not enough eager numbers of militia willing to take up arms for the Earl's cause, so he decided to enter into a self-imposed exile primarily due to his increasingly fail physical and mental health. Shaftesbury had the sense to know when he had lost and he set sail for the Protestant, Dutch Republic from Gravesend. He probably suspected that he would never see England again. He arrived late November 1682, at the Dutch port of Brielle from where he would travel to his final journey's end, Amsterdam, arriving on the 2 December, 1682. On 17 January 1683, only weeks after fleeing England, Shaftesbury drew up his final will and testament and died four days later on 21 January. Robert Ferguson was with his friend when he passed away. The earl's corpse was shipped back to England, where he would be interred in Wimborne, Dorset, in accordance with his wishes expressed in his new will.

Shaftesbury may not have been a military man like Monmouth, but he was an extraordinarily talented politician, who survived dangerous political crises through changing his political alliance several times during his career. His greatest skill was to do this while retaining the trust of his new ally, whomever that might be, which was a great political achievement during the seventeenth century, when politics could become deadly. Shaftesbury, like the rest of his early Whig colleagues, was passionate about his ideals, which led him to becoming a leading figure in the Exclusionist cause. But even with these ambitious passions, Shaftesbury remained logical and level headed; attributes that may have helped the rebellion plotters immediately after the death of Charles II. Had he not become ill and died, Shaftesbury's influence may have changed the outcome of Monmouth's story, or at the very least given his rebellion the best chance of succeeding.

Frustrated due to a lack of ability to make changes legally through parliament, the extreme Exclusionists decided to take matters into their own hands and remove both the king and the Duke of York in an assassination plot; thus leaving Monmouth to be their puppet monarch. The consequences of this plot included the arrest and execution of many hardcore Exclusionists, increased distrust and suspicion of Monmouth from both his father and his uncle, and Monmouth being finally forced into exile.

The Rye House plot brought the Duke of Monmouth close to the fate of some of his friends; it was his wife whom he had cheated on and was virtually estranged from, who would beg for his life with his father, the king. It is fair to surmise that this was the point where Monmouth's relationship with his father had completely changed; Monmouth was no longer on the pedestal Charles had put him on, he had lost his father's admiration and respect, and was no longer a court favourite. The foiled plot would also seal York's unfavourable opinion of his nephew and consequently this would set Monmouth firmly on the road to his doom.

The plot takes its name from the location where the assassination should have taken place. Rye House was a manor located in the southern county of Hertfordshire and at the time of the plot, it was being rented by a former Parliamentarian and supporter of Cromwell, Richard Rumbold. In the lead up to the would be assassination, Rye House, a solid property surrounded by a moat, was being prepared with supplies, weapons and men. During the planning, both the insurrection and assassination were discussed, but not all in the group were happy to commit or be part of regicide. Rye House's location was excellent for such a plot as it was just far away from Tory-held London and remote enough for the plotters to hope that their dastardly plan had a better chance of being kept secret and succeeding.

The detail of the plot was to assassinate Charles and the Duke of York on their way back to Whitehall after attending the races at Newmarket. The plot was spoiled when the royal party left Newmarket just over a week earlier than planned, following a major fire that broke out in the town. The fire was reported in the *London Gazette* at the time:

> Newmarket March 23. Last night between nine and ten a clock a fire happened here which began in a stable yard and burn so violently the wind being high, that in a few hours above half the town was laid in ashes. Their majesties removed to earl of Suffolk's house.[44]

The fire at Newmarket was also recorded by the MP and historian Narcissus Luttrell, who wrote in his diary:

> On 22 instant at night between nine and ten a fire happened at the town of Newmarket, which began in a stable by the carelessness of a groom taking tobacco: the wind being high it burnt quiet furiously that it consumed half the town... but his majesties house received no damage.[45]

The plot was exposed when one of its own collaborators, Joshua Keeling, defected and exposed the scheme to the Secretary of State, Sir Leoline Jenkins. Having exposed the failed plot, Keeling expected a pardon for the part he had played in the treasonous assassination scheme. The conspiracy to assassinate the king and his brother became public knowledge on 12 July 1683. Why Keeling decided to became a turncoat and inform the authorities is unknown, but an educated guess would be that he felt the plot was likely to be discovered, thus thought by turning informant he had a chance of keeping his life.

Two of the plotters, Robert West and Robert Ferguson, later independently claimed that even if the scheme had happened at the correct time, the plotters would not have been ready. One of the main problems was that the conspirators were lacking agreement on key objectives of the plot. Many were unhappy with the idea of regicide and favoured rebellion. There was also disharmony about what should happen after the event; should England be thrown back into a political state of a republic, or should there be a monarch in the form of Protestant Monmouth or William of Orange? This confusion is shown in a letter from Earl of Ormond to the Earl of Arran, dated 7 July 1683:

> Ever since about midsummer day, we have been satisfied of the truth of the information first given of a design laid for the assassination of the King and Duke and for the raising of a rebellion in England and Scotland and although I make them two designs because it does not appear that all who were in at the rebellion were in for the assassination or privy to it.[46]

One of the ideas was that a rebellion would start in England and subsequently to trigger a second rebellion in Scotland, under the leadership of Archibald Campbell, 9th Earl of Argyll. This idea of a two-pronged rebellion simultaneously attacking Scotland and England can later be seen as the blue print for Monmouth's rebellion; the details in the plans are so alike, that they even involved the same people.

As the plot unravelled and men came forward, hoping confessions would literally save their necks, others who were slower in coming forward were implemented in the planning of this treasonous plan. Twelve people were executed as a result of their involvement with the Rye House Plot: Sir Thomas Armstrong, MP for Stafford; John Ayloffe; Henry Cornish, Sheriff of the City of London; Elizabeth Gaunt; James Holloway;

Baillie Jerviswood; Richard Nelthorpe; Richard Rumbold; John Rouse; William Russell, Lord Russell, MP for Bedfordshire; Algernon Sidney and Thomas Walcot.

Seven of the accused were sentenced to the traitor's death of being hanged, drawn and quartered. Jerviswood and Nelthorpe were merely hanged and Elizabeth Gaunt was burned at the stake. As members of the nobility, Lord Russell and Algernon Sidney were beheaded.

Other men who were arrested, but not sentenced to death for their part or suspected part in the plot, were as follows: Sir Samuel Barnardiston (also fined £6,000); Henry Booth, 1st Earl of Warrington; Archibald Campbell, 9th Earl of Argyll; Paul Foley, MP for Herefordshire; Thomas Grey, 2nd Earl of Stamford; John Hampden, MP for Wendover (also fined £40,000); William Howard 3rd Baron Howard of Escrick; Matthew Mead; Aaron Smith; Sir John Trenchard, MP for Taunton and Sir John Wildman.

From the list above, several names are important to Monmouth's rebellion. Archibald Campbell, 9th Earl of Argyll, led the Scottish rebellion prior to Monmouth arriving in the West Country, and Sir John Trenchard, MP for Taunton, where Monmouth was declared king during his rebellion. More conspirators fled into self-imposed exile in the Netherlands, where they were highly likely to have met with the duke during his exile prior to his rebellion. It is probable that these men continued to help the remaining Exclusionists with their plans. Also involved were: Sir John Cochrane; Robert Ferguson; Ford Grey, 3rd Baron Grey of Werke; Patrick Hume, 1st Earl of Marchmont; John Locke; John Lovelace, 3rd Baron Lovelace; David Melville, 3rd Earl of Leven; Edward Norton and Nathaniel Wade.

One of the saddest casualties of this failed plot was Arthur Capel, the Earl of Essex, who cut his own throat in the Tower of London. He carried out this grim method of suicide in order for his family to be able to inherit his titles and land, which would have been forfeited by the crown and state if he was executed.

Charles, the Duke of York and the Tories all chased for the convictions of the plotters, but by doing so they were undermining the respect people had for the monarchy; for the king was permitting the law to be used to ensure a political pivot in his favour, only sparing those whom he had an interest in keeping alive. One of those who it was not in the king's interest to keep alive was Algernon Sidney, who's death was recorded in a letter from Sir Robert Reading:

> Col. Sidney died resolutely enough, as was expected. He was
> not eight minutes on the scaffold and was dead before the

guards came upon Tower Hill. He made no speech but gave a paper to the sheriffs which will be printed on Monday.[47]

The Duke of Monmouth can be blamed for the fact that Sidney ended up on the block, rather than being banished, as can be seen in another letter from Sir Robert Reading:

> To prevent all these evils, the King caused the Duke of Monmouth to declare that all … evidence was true … and a paper will be out in print two days signed by the said Duke to this purpose…Sidney, of whom there was some deliberation to banish is now appointed to die Friday, and certainly dies for his friends indiscretion.[48]

No matter how Charles behaved in the aftermath of the discovery of the plot, there is no denying that the safety of the king and his heir had been threatened, and there was now fear of another civil war. The law had to be upheld and that required making examples of the men who had been involved in the treasonous venture. This in turn was supposed to act as a preventative measure to future political plotters; it is a shame that the Duke of Monmouth did not take note. The Whigs felt that the Tories had used the plot as a good excuse to get rid of all the Duke of York's enemies, and to punish the Exclusionists' behaviour and avenge the Whigs' role in bringing about the execution of poor William Howard, Lord Stafford.

Several historians agree that, although the Duke of Monmouth was embroiled in the Rye House plot, he would not have agreed to being involved in or agreed to the assassination of both his father and uncle:

> The Duke of Monmouth and the rest pressed them to put things in speedy execution, [but] ... the Duke of Monmouth had been very backward and had used such expressions as these to him, as how it be expected he should draw his sword against his Majesty, it was unnatural for him to do it.[49]

Even though Monmouth may not have been prepared to take up arms against his own father, Charles must have felt wounded by the knowledge that he was involved in such a treacherous scheme. Charles knew he had to tread carefully in how he dealt with his wayward eldest son, in order to maintain good relations with his brother. The king did seek reconciliation with Monmouth, although this was mostly due to encouragement from the Earl of Halifax, George Saville, and Monmouth's wife.

Charles also wanted to approach Monmouth in order to gain the evidence needed to convict the remaining conspirators of the plot. Monmouth's wife, Anne, wrote a letter to the king on her husband's behalf:

> Since I am so unhappy as to have no hopes of seeing Your Majestie to ask your leave to deliver this letter to you, I had no other way of putting it into your hands...I was the more encouraged to do because he writes to me that, except Your Majestie be resolved on his ruin he is sure he can at this time be serviceable to you, so I hope Your Majestie will not refuse to accept of that entire submission and great penitence from him, which your goodness would not perhaps deny to another man. I beg your Majesty will not be displeased with me since I doubt not but that his letter is of consequence because he pressed me deliver it with all speed to Your Majestie.[50]

While the duchess wrote to the king, Halifax advised the duke how best to approach him. He recommended that Monmouth write to his father and show reconciliation to his uncle, York by requesting that the Duke of York himself should be the one to reintroduce him at court, should he be permitted to return. Due to the influences of the Earl of Halifax and the Duchess of Monmouth, the duke was able to meet Charles away from the court on 24 October. Unfortunately, the duke, who should have been in exile, was spotted and rumour soon circulated that Monmouth was back in London. This did not amuse the Duke of York. Charles knew that he needed to arrange a truce between his son and brother, so a second incognito meeting between the king and Monmouth was arranged on 4 November, in which Charles tutored his son on how to pacify York.

A plan was hatched; Charles solicited the help of Queen Catherine who went to speak with the Duchess of York and together they embarked upon vanquishing the Duke of York's justified suspicion of the Duke of Monmouth. The second part of the plan was that Monmouth would write a convincing letter to the king confessing his role in the plot. Reluctantly, Monmouth signed his name to this letter on 15 November.

Ten days later, Monmouth arrived at court in the early evening of 25 November. He went directly to the Secretary of State's office and told him calmly that he had come to prostrate himself at the king's feet. What happened in this meeting was recorded in the Calender of State Papers:

> Yesterday the Duke of Monmouth surrendered himself to the secretary Jenkins and desired to speak alone with the King and the Duke, which was granted. He first threw himself at his majesties feet acknowledging his guilt and his share in the conspiracy and asked his pardon, then confessed himself guilty to the Duke, asked his pardon also.[51]

Monmouth was escorted to his former residence at court known as the Cockpit. The following day, the king acted on his promise of a pardon for his son at a full meeting of the Privy Council. The last part of the carefully orchestrated public apology of the Duke of Monmouth happened on the same day, when Monmouth called upon his uncle's chambers and humbly requested his forgiveness. This was then repeated more publicly in the king's quarters at court.

The fragile truce between the two dukes would not last, and the cause of this broken peace was a scandalous and poorly-worded report in the *London Gazette,* which insinuated that Monmouth confessed fully to his role in the plot, undermining all the carefully-written letters and coaching from Halifax.

> The Duke caused that part of the *Gazette* of that day which related to himself to be read over and told them that it was all false and that he had been to the King about it and that it should be altered in the following *Gazette* and that he bade them acquaint all their friends that nothing of it was true.[52]

When York discovered that Monmouth had denied that he had fully confessed to playing a role within the Rye House Plot, he would come to regret forgiving his rebellious nephew. This was because York had only been persuaded to forgive Monmouth by the king, who had given the impression that Monmouth had fully confessed to his 'involvement' in the failed assassination plot against them both. Charles thought the best solution to restore the truce between his son and York was for Monmouth to sign a public declaration stating his involvement and subsequent guilt. This in turn would not undermine the evidence of those already convicted of their involvement in the crime, while placating York at the same time.

A new document was drawn up with careful consideration for the wording by Secretary Jenkins and Halifax. It was then up to Halifax and the Duchess of Monmouth to try and convince the duke to sign the public declaration. When Halifax presented Monmouth with the declaration he told him that it must be signed and to leave no room for debate. Eventually, Monmouth co-operated and signed, much to Halifax's and the duchess' relief. Monmouth's reluctance to sign was that he feared by doing so, he would sentence his friends to death for their part in the plot.

This fear of implicating his friends caused Monmouth to go to the king the next day and request the signed declaration back. Charles listened to his son and reassured him that he would not be required to personally testify against any of his friends during their trials. Deep down, Monmouth knew the document was enough to do that for him. Charles was then confronted with his distressed and overwrought son who begged upon his knees and asked his father for the biggest favour he could beg of him. The pitiful sight of his son was enough for Charles to hand Monmouth the document. By doing so, the king was left with very little choice in terms of how to deal with his son. After all, Monmouth would need to be punished for his part in the plot and so he would have to send his obeisant son away from court and into exile.

The tragic irony for Monmouth's loyal gesture to protect his friends did not ultimately save them from their fates. The next day, 7 December, as the duke was being ordered to leave his father's court indefinitely, his friend and comrade Algernon Sidney was meeting a swift end upon the scaffold.

Monmouth's departure from court and country was swift. He returned to his marital home of Moor Park to gather what he needed to travel and headed towards the European mainland. He waited for the last of the Rye House plotters to be tried before he returned to England to arrange for his possessions to be shipped to Europe. When the plotter, John Hamden was tried in February, Monmouth was, as he feared he would be, called to give witness against his friend. A cursory hunt for Monmouth was carried out but when he wasn't found, the trial went ahead. Hampden escaped with a fine without Monmouth's testimony, as grounds for High Treason could not be proved. Monmouth discreetly returned in March to settle his affairs in England.

> I saw one of the Duke of Monmouth's servants in disguise, so
> I pretended not to be well Saturday night…here are 13 horses
> of the Duke of Monmouth…the horses are shipped today but
> I think the wind will not carry them.[53]

For the first part of his exile on the continent, Monmouth was located in Brussels. From the Flemish city, the duke moved on to The Hague, the royal court of his cousins, William of Orange and Princess Mary, where he stayed as their guest. His exile was hardly punishing as he was given nice comfortable houses and was royally entertained at balls and parties. He even had the company of his long term mistress and true love, Henrietta Maria Wentworth, to help him through his exile. While in Europe, Monmouth also visited the Brandenburg capital, Berlin, where he was warmly welcomed by the Elector, who nevertheless said he received the duke as the king's son, not as the Duke of Monmouth.

Unsurprisingly, the Duke of York become angry with his son-in-law for making Monmouth comfortable and welcomed during his exile. This frustration at Monmouth's comfortable exile is reflected in a letter he wrote to The Hague: 'I was sorry to find by letters which came over by the same post that the Duke of Monmouth had been with you there.'[54]

Sunday, 1 February 1685, was the last normal evening in the life of Charles II. It was spent, as much of his reign was, with a beautiful woman who was not his wife, gambling and having fun. The mistress in question was his beloved Fubbs, Louise de Kérouaille, the Duchess of Portsmouth. They were enjoying the evening in her apartments, gambling after a hearty meal which included rich goose eggs.

Later, after Charles had retired to his bed, he spent the night tossing and turning, which was out of character for the king, who was normally a sound sleeper. In the morning, he was said to have had a complexion that was described as pale and sickly. After emerging from his privy closet, it was evident that Charles had suffered a stroke as his speech had been effected. Unsure of what to do, his servants continued with his morning routine of getting him ready for the day. Just as he was being prepared for a shave, the king howled like a banshee and passed out.

The doctor that first attended the king was Sir Edmund King, who administered the seventeenth century's favourite treatment, bleeding, and took an astonishing 16 fl oz of blood. Sir Edmund King would later be paid a staggering £1,000 for this task; an enormous reward when considering his patient did not recover from his treatment. While the king was having his royal blood let, the Privy Council was informed that Charles was gravely ill. In his diary entry for the day, John Evelyn noted that:

> By God's providence, Dr King (that excellent chirurgeon as well as physician) had not been accidentally present to let

him blood (having his lancet in his pocket) his Majesty had certainly died that moment.[55]

Sir Edmund King was not the only medic to treat Charles. As news of the king's sickness spread, a steady stream of quacks entered the royal presence to attempt to 'treat' the monarch. Among the useless treatments Charles received for his stroke were having his head shaved and being bled again, consequently losing a further 8 fl oz of blood. Charles must have had a good constitution, as a few hours later he had regained his ability to speak coherently and requested to see the queen.

As a precaution, all the nation's ports were closed and no ships or vessels were allowed in or out of the country for any reason. This was done so that news of the king's condition did not reach the Duke of Monmouth or William of Orange, who may in turn have used this knowledge to their political advantage. Although this may have been the last act of love between a father and his son, it was more likely to have been done to protect the Duke of York's interest, as the heir to the throne. Regardless of how delayed the news of Charles' illness and subsequent death was in reaching Monmouth, his chosen path had already been decided and fate's die cast.

The recovery of Charles was short lived. On Tuesday, 3 February, in the presence of no less than twelve doctors, the king was thought to have had another stroke. The quacks' treatments were renewed with eager abandonment, causing Charles great distress and pain, in their mission to rid the king's body of evil humours. Evelyn tells us:

> He was cupped, let blood in both jugulars, and both vomit and purges which so relieved him … they prescribed the famous Jesuit Powder; but this made him worse and some very able doctors who were present did not think it a fever but the effect of his frequent bleeding and other sharp operations used by them about his head.[56]

Before he finally breathed his last, Charles is said to have converted to Roman Catholicism with the help of the queen's chaplain, Father Huddleston. Huddleston was the priest who had helped Charles when he was on the run following the Battle of Worcester. As reward for his assistance at that difficult time, Huddleston had been granted the position of queen's chaplain.

Royal etiquette meant that some of the most important people in Charles' life were not with him at his end. The two mistresses that Charles remembered on his deathbed were Nell Gwyn and the Duchess of Portsmouth, whom he asked his brother James to look after. However, John Evelyn noted that he did not mention Monmouth, his people or the church:

> He also recommended to him the care of his natural children, all except the Duke of Monmouth, now in Holland and in his displeasure. He entreated the Queen to pardon him (not without cause); who little before had sent a bishop to excuse her not more frequent visiting him, in regard of her excessive grief.... he spoke to the Duke to be kind to the Duchess of Cleveland, and especially Portsmouth and that Nelly might not starve.[57]

On 9 February, Charles asked for the curtains in his room to be drawn back so that he could watch the sunrise. By 9 am he had lost the ability to speak, and just before midday he breathed his last. The Duke of York was now King James II and the first Catholic to sit on the throne of Britain since the disastrous reign of Mary I. The remaining extremist Whig supporters in exile immediately used the news of Charles' death as the excuse to start planning a rebellion against the new Catholic king.

Upon the news of Charles' death, William of Orange found himself in an awkward and embarrassing situation. He was technically harbouring a treasonous fugitive, one that the new king and his father-in-law, James II considered a threat to his royal person and the state. News of Charles' death finally reached William at The Hague on 20 February 1685 and the unpleasant task of breaking the news to both Mary and Monmouth was left to William. The Duke of Monmouth's grief for his father was heard on the street, according to contemporary accounts, as he wept within his quarters.[58] That evening, William met with Monmouth for several hours requesting that he leave The Hague, as well as offering his royal cousin help with how best to try and regain favour with his uncle, James II. William had prepared a missive for Monmouth; it was addressed to the new King James seeking forgiveness and swearing obedience and fidelity. The missive was never sent, Monmouth left The Hague and his cousins two days after hearing the news of his father's death. Monmouth now found himself in a situation where no one could pacify his unpredictable and stubborn uncle. The enormity of his grief for his estranged father may have also been exaggerated by fear of his future.

Monmouth and Henrietta Maria's first stop after leaving William and Mary's court was Rotterdam. From there, they moved on to Brussels but the vindictive and vengeful James II had ordered the Spanish governor, the Marquis de Grana, to inform Monmouth to leave the Spanish Netherlands territories, of which Brussels was part, upon his arrival.

The lovers would head to Antwerp and it is here that Monmouth and the Earl of Argyll, first reconnected. Argyll had not learned his lesson from the failed Rye House Plot. He also refused to see James as king and still referred to him as the 'Duke of York'. He felt that if they were to succeed in dethroning James, action was required sooner rather than later; before James had established himself properly as a monarch and caused too much damage to Protestant Britain.

For the first time in his adult life, Monmouth was happy and seemed unwilling to risk his happiness with Henrettia without a great deal of persuasion. Rather, it was men such as Argyll, Grey and Ferguson who relentlessly badgered the grieving Monmouth into taking action against his uncle, the king. Now that he had found the woman he loved and lost his father, the man who had loved him and had protected him from the axe, the time would have been right for him to leave Whitehall and its exclusion politics behind and to please himself. Another option was to go abroad. Europe presented plenty of opportunities for a military man of his reputation, should he wish to seek adventure, and if he chose to continue to be a soldier, life in exile could have been comfortable if he decided to settle down.

However, during the spring of 1685, Monmouth, became a wondering exile. His uncle had made it plain to his associates on the continent that he wanted to know the movements of his nephew and was deeply suspicious of him. Eventually, Monmouth and Henrietta Maria lived in Gouda, in the south of the Netherlands, and for a while the pair were happy and settled into their lives together. His former comrades however felt differently and it was inevitable that it would only be a matter of time before Monmouth would try and pacify them and be drawn into their plots and plans once again. Their chosen method was to use the love of his life, Henrietta, to persuade Monmouth to rejoin them.

Chapter 12

The Beginning of the End

Whence comes it that religion and the laws
Should more be Absalom's than David's cause?
His old instructor, e're he lost his place,
Was never thought indu'd with so much Grace:
Good heav'ns, how faction can a Patriot paint!
My Rebel ever proves my people's saint:
Would *they* impose an Heir upon the Throne?

The above extract taken from John Dryden's epic poem, *Absalom and Achitophel* gives a preview of Monmouth's fall from grace through the last few months of his life. Using religion as motivation and justification for his actions, and encouraged by those with ulterior and selfish motives, such as Archibald Campbell, 9th Earl of Argyll, Monmouth turned against his uncle, King James II. He became the people's rebel and subsequently their Protestant Martyr following his failure and execution in the summer of 1685.

As early as two weeks after Charles II had died, a prophecy found in the Calendar of State Papers forecasted a battle between the two Jameses; James Duke of Monmouth and the former Duke of York, now King James II:

> They say two Dukes shall fight for the crown of England, which two dukes they term to be the Duke of York now King, the other the Duke of Monmouth and they say that in this battle the Duke of York shall be slain and the crown party totally routed but there shall be several battles fought before this, yet this battle is supposed to be fought in this year eighty five, by which they do propose to themselves that the King will not live long.[59]

The prophecy suggests that there was much popular support for Monmouth and that the new king would be the loser. However, the reality of such feelings are rarely accurate, and in this case, although James II did in fact have a short reign, it was not his nephew who brought his ascendancy to an abrupt end, but his daughter and son-in-law, William of Orange, who would have that privilege.

The Monmouth Rebellion was not meant to be a solo effort, rather the plan was that it would be part of a two-pronged attack. The attack on James II would start first with a rebellion in Scotland, led by the disgraced and exiled Archibald Campbell, 9th Earl of Argyll, followed by a second attack led by the Duke of Monmouth starting in the south-west where his support was strongest, before moving towards London and into the city. The second attack by Monmouth would ideally happen once the Scottish capital of Edinburgh was secured by the Earl of Argyll.

In order to understand why the Earl of Argyll wanted to get involved with Monmouth, it is important to look to both the man and his politics. At the beginning of Charles II's reign, Argyll had been found guilty of treason. However, in 1663 he managed to have his sentence reduced and his hereditary lands restored to his family. Shortly after that, in the summer of 1664, he found himself on the rise as he became one of the men of the Scottish Privy Council. Argyll remained true and loyal to Charles and even supported the king in passing the Scottish Succession Act in 1681. This was somewhat ironic as it would have allowed the Catholic Duke of York the right to succeed his brother on the Scottish throne, Scotland being, of course, the ancestral homeland of the Stuart royal family. The point at which Argyll turned from loyal subject to traitor, was when the English parliament tried to introduce the Scottish Test Act.

Like the previous Test Acts passed in England, in 1673 and 1678 respectively, the Scottish Test Act of 1681 was introduced in order to show that the king upheld the protection of the Protestant faith and expected all his civil servants in public office to prove their commitment to the Protestant faith, and the monarch, through an oath. Argyll tried to stop the act being passed within the Scottish parliament, but the bill still passed by just seven votes. There were exemptions to the Test Act: the king, the Duke of York and his subsequent sons and heirs (if and when they arrived). As the Duke of York rejected the oath when he was the heir presumptive, the future James II was omitting an oath to preserve the Protestant faith within Scotland. Understandably, this fuelled fears of the prospect of York inheriting the throne among the Protestant bishops and clergy within the Scottish Kirk, as well as the ruling Protestant nobility.

Argyll objected to the idea that Scotland's subjects had to swear an oath to a religion they already supported and yet their monarch would not swear the same oath to support the very faith he was supposedly the head of. That Charles' heir and brother, who was not even of the Protestant communion, was also exempt added insult to the injury, and was seen as a bigger threat to the Protestants of Scotland, as well as proving a step too far for the Earl of Argyll. This was the principal reason why Argyll refused to comply with the Act and in failing to swear his oath, he once again found himself guilty of treason. In December 1681, he escaped from his jail within Edinburgh Castle and fled into exile on the European mainland, where he remained within the Protestant territory of the United Provinces. It had been the then Duke of York who had called the Scottish parliament in Charles' name and it was with him that Argyll felt most strongly aggrieved. Monmouth and Argyll now shared a common grievance and enemy: James II.

While in exile after his escape, the Earl of Argyll had started to plot and plan a rebellion within Scotland in response to his anger about the Scottish Test Act. Argyll had been introduced to Monmouth while the Exclusionists were planning the Rye House Plot in 1682. He believed it would be to his benefit if the duke carried out a second rebellion in England after he [Argyll] had secured Edinburgh. It would also mean that he could help orchestrate the new government in Edinburgh, one that suited his plans and interests in Scotland.

In the months before his father's death, Monmouth, together with the Earl of Argyll, plotted. However, these plans would have been fast forwarded and changed due to unexpected death of Charles. Apart from the suspected stroke that Charles had suffered in 1679, the king was still extremely active and in good health, both mentally and physically, in the approach of his last illness and subsequent death. Charles II was only 54 years old at the time of his death, which was reasonably young for a man of that time, especially one who had access to good food and maintained an active lifestyle.

For a joint rebellion to have a better chance of being successful, the timings of both ventures needed to be well-timed and executed. The Earl of Argyll was to land in Scotland first in order to preoccupy and confuse James' army and keep them distracted, while the Duke of Monmouth landed in the south-west of England and started a second uprising. If all went to plan, by this time the Earl of Argyll would have captured and have full control of Edinburgh, which in turn would mean that smaller insurgencies could start in other places, allowing Monmouth to move his volunteer supporters towards London. For this grand plan to succeed, it would need a popular figurehead, and it would help if he was handsome, dashing and charming, and be able to glean support from Exclusionist sympathisers and Whigs throughout the south of England. Monmouth also hoped that his cause would attract support from Protestant dissenters, with the assumption that they also feared the king would start persecuting them as he converted England back to Rome. However, history and the fate of these two men worked out very differently.

The standard carried by the Earl of Argyll's supporters bore the message: 'For God and Religion, Against Poperie, Tyrannie, Arbitrary Government and Erastianism'. The Essence of Argyll's motto is that he and his supporters were not only anti-Catholic but also against the principle of Erastianism - meaning the state is superior to the church within society. For Argyll, God was first and the king second and the monarchy needed to reflect and preserve the Protestant faith of the people they governed. In other words, Argyll opposed everything that the Duke of York was and represented.

The final details of the invasion plans were drawn up in Amsterdam in April 1685. However, Argyll and Monmouth disagreed on when to invade: Argyll wanted to attack James prior to his coronation, which was due to be held on 23 April, St Georges Day. This unfortunately would have left both parties only days to plan, mobilise, arm, sail and attack. Unsurprisingly, Monmouth, with his military training and experience, disagreed with Argyll. He understood planning was key to their endeavour succeeding. There was also the predicament that, unlike Argyll, Monmouth did not have access to the same level of income required for such a large operation as launching a rebellion. Monmouth had not had as long as Argyll to prepare, gather weapons and men, or arrange the necessary logistics. Even if Monmouth had had easy access to such support and income, he knew that he would require time to give the men the basic and rudimentary military training needed in order for him to have a fighting chance of winning against local militia and the well-trained English standing army.

The plotters did not manage to start their attack on James II before he was crowned, but they set the wheels in motion at a faster speed than Monmouth was comfortable with. The details of their plans stated that Monmouth would set sail for the south-west of England no later than six days after Argyll had sailed for Scotland. From there he was supposed to move through the West Country, taking the cities of Bristol and Gloucester. It was hoped that by doing that he would have access to more supporters and supplies to fight the king's troops, as well as leaving London open and more vulnerable for the Whigs to seize the city ready for Monmouth's eventual arrival. This plan was reliant on the Earl of Argyll succeeding in Scotland and capturing Edinburgh as well as Monmouth attracting the same level of support he had gathered on his progresses in 1682 and 1683. This meant that the general populace would be happy and willing to risk turning against their new king, which would primarily depend on how worried they were about his Catholicism and how it would affect them. Many people were within living memory of the bloody Civil Wars; would they be prepared to commit treason and risk death by hanging for a charming, handsome duke?

The Earl of Argyll set sail for his native country, heading for the west coast of Scotland on 2 May 1685. Initially, the party of rebels stopped in Orkney on 6 May. They were, however, not welcomed when the authorities were alerted to their arrival on the island. They then continued their venture by heading to the west coast, sailing around the north of Scotland where the earl and his supporters eventually arrived off the coast of Mull on 11 May. One of the first objectives Argyll had to undertake upon landing was to recruit some more men for his cause and he began this recruitment drive on the Isle of Islay. The Register of the Privy Council of Scotland records a proclamation commanding a levy of Scottish forces to prepare for the impending invasion by the earl:

> Late Earl of Argyll hath not only consulted and concurred with the English conspirators in their late treasonable plot against the King's person…but hath been eminently active … the King being obliged by the law … to established lieutenancies in the shires of Argyll and Tarbit for preventing and suppressing the projects and seditions intended by the said late Archibald.[60]

Unfortunately, the Earl of Argyll grossly over-estimated the support he was hoping to receive within his native Scotland. He had asked his son to recruit men from their own tenants, but very few answered their landlords' treasonous call to arms. Also, both Argyll and Monmouth had lost the element of surprise to their invasions. This meant that James was therefore able to prepare for the two invading parties and anticipate what they were hoping to achieve through their planned duel attack. James would also have made sure to protect London and prepare the troops he needed to defeat both Argyll and Monmouth.

Another problem Argyll faced was that he struggled to keep discipline with the men he had been able to gather. Discipline within any army is vital for any operation or invasion to succeed, as can be seen throughout history, from the Romans right up to Oliver Cromwell's New Model Army. Ironically, the earl was hoping to recruit a large section of his support from the Covenanters; the same Presbyterian sect that the Duke of Monmouth had defeated at the Battle of Bothwell Bridge in 1679.

Argyll issued a declaration claiming that James II had caused the death of Charles and that the rightful heir was in fact James, Duke of Monmouth not James, Duke of York. James II had taken the precaution of sending loyal royalist troops to areas that had the strongest support for the Earl of Argyll. With no immediate battle, the undisciplined men began to lose faith in their leader and they started to mutiny and desert. The rag-tag army moved from Bute, to Corval, in Argyllshire, and on to Greenock, before moving to Inveraray. From there, Argyll and his men headed to the garrison of Eileen Gheirrig, before making a temporary base at Ardkinglass Castle. It was not long before they decided to return back to Eileen Gheirrig. By this point, Argyll had lost the ships that he had used to sail from Europe to Scotland, and the earl now had no way of escape open to him, or anyway of communicating to Monmouth that things had gone wrong.

With few options left, Argyll headed to the lowlands of Scotland with the remaining support he had for his cause. En route south, he found himself in a favourable position to attack the royal troops. His comrades managed to persuaded him not to fight the royal forces, but instead to make their way towards Scotland's second city, Glasgow. At this point, Argyll only had a mere 2,000 men left willing to risk their lives to support him. Following skirmishes with the king's troops, not to mention deaths and desertions, Argyll soon found himself left with only a handful of men, one of which was his son John. The Earl of Argyll must have realised he was defeated and at this point, the men decided to separate to avoid drawing attention to themselves and in the hope of avoiding capture.

On 18 June, Argyll himself was captured when he came up against a group of royal militia. He went to shoot the men who captured him but when he pulled the trigger of his gun, the powder had become damp and it failed to go off. The Scottish rebellion had officially come to an end. Where and how Argyll was detained is recorded in the following extract from Narcissus Luttrell:

> The rebels in Scotland march towards Sterling [sic] …and attempting to cross the river Clyde, the kings forces overtook them and dispersed them presently: Argyll himself was taken.[61]

Argyll's arrest and those of his fellow rebels can also be traced through the Scottish Privy Council papers. On 18 June, Argyll's captor was rewarded £50 for his efforts:

> Argyll is expected as a prisoner and orders are given for his passage to the castle…. the cashkeeper to pay John Riddell, webster, £50 sterling for apprehending Argyll.[62]

Two days after his capture, Argyll was brought Edinburgh, where he was questioned and then held in prison. He was allowed a visit from both his wife and his sister, Lady Lothian. On 30 June 1685, he was brought to Edinburgh's place of execution, where he faced death by an early form of the guillotine, known by the Scots as the Maiden. He declined to make a final speech, but did leave a written account, that can now be found in the Scottish Privy Register. It quotes many biblical passages, however, the last two paragraphs are the most telling about his motives for his role in the rebellion.

> I do freely forgive all that directly and indirectly have been the cause of bringing me to this place … I pray God send peace and truth to these three kingdoms and countenance and encourage the glorious light of the gospel and restrain the spirit of profanity, atheism, supersition, popery and persecution… I said that at my death I would pray that there should never want one of the royal family to be defender o the true ancient apostolical catholical protestant faith, which now I do.[63]

It is said on the scaffold before meeting his maker, Argyll joked saying that he was about to meet 'the sweetest maiden he had ever kissed.'[64]

At the time of Argyll's execution, Monmouth had started his own rebellion in the West Country. He had no idea that his fellow rebel in arms had lost his rebellion, and consequently his head. When the news of Argyll's death and defeat reached Monmouth, it was at a critical time of his invasion, when he too found himself in trouble. Maybe this was when Monmouth saw his own fate and decided to fight to the end and go out with the dignity of a soldier.

On 11 June 1685, Monmouth landed at Lyme Regis, Dorset, with around 150 men. Among those he brought with him were his fellow exiles who had escaped punishment after the Rye House Plot, including Lord Ford Grey, Nathaniel Wade and Robert Ferguson. Upon landing at Lyme Regis, the first miscalculation Monmouth had made became reality when he could not recruit large numbers of Protestant dissenters from the area to his cause.

The reason the Duke had assumed that there was this level of support waiting for him was due in part to the positive response he had seen during his progresses within the region a couple of years before. There was no communication between himself and the Earl of Argyll, but Monmouth was hoping that his fellow comrade had managed to capture Edinburgh by this point. Monmouth knew timing was important to their plan; the closer the timing of Edinburgh's being under Argyll's control to his landing in Dorset, the greater the chance of his invasion being successful. This would be due to James' troops being preoccupied in Scotland and in theory, making it easier for Monmouth and his men to move towards London and a Whig-secured city, ready to welcome him as king. Monmouth, however, did not know that the element of surprise required for this to work had been lost and that his uncle knew of both Argyll's and his invasions. With hindsight, the rebellion was doomed from the start.

Two days after the Duke of Monmouth landed in Lyme Regis, James issued a Proclamation from Whitehall, warning the people of England against Monmouth.

> Three proclamations one for the seizing of James Duke of Monmouth and his accomplices; The other for the suppression of a traitorous declaration published by the said Duke of Monmouth aforesaid; and the last for a reward of five thousand pounds for the taking and securing of his body either dead or alive.[65]

This had little or no effect on the men and woman of the West Country, where Monmouth was currently located. For them, the duke represented a Protestant hope against the Catholic king. It also helped that Monmouth was young, handsome, brave and heroic and so appealed to the women of the town.

Although James had known of the planned invasions, at the start of Monmouth's invasion, his threat must have given the king legitimate reason to be concerned. James had a national army of 10,000 men, as well as access to local militia, who although trained, had little or no experience of real fighting. He needed to keep the militia where each unit was based, so that if local insurrections broke out they were on the spot to deal with the problem swiftly and hopefully effectively. It would be their job to try to contain the rioting and to stop it from spreading. However, James was also running the risk of the trained and equipped militia deserting his side for the charismatic Monmouth and his Protestant cause. It must have been a very worrying time for the new king.

Instead of marching his men straight to London, the Duke of Monmouth decided to march his followers towards Somerset in order to gather more men to join his growing army of volunteers. Monmouth approached the town of Bridport on 14 June 1685, where his men engaged in a fight with the local royal militia. At this point, the Earl of Argyll was still attempting to get to Edinburgh. There was a threat that if Argyll was not captured soon, the fighting in Scotland could have crossed Hadrian's Wall and spread into the north of England.

If the king had sent too many troops to Dorset and the south-west, it would have allowed those left in London to form the impression that it was safe to rise in favour of the duke. The rebellion was evenly matched strategically and although there was a difference in numbers and resources, luck was also a principle element in the rebellion, and either side could have succeeded at this point. The city of Salisbury was of key importance to the outcome of this balance of power; if the king's men had managed to reach it, roughly six days hard march from London, it is thought it would be impossible for them to return to the capital to stop London from declaring for Monmouth's cause. The timing was vital; getting it wrong would also give Monmouth ten days in order to prepare his new and raw recruits.[66]

Monmouth had both the experience and reputation of being a great military man, which was something James had seen for himself. He must have feared that his nephew had more than a good chance of winning his rebellion and taking the crown from him. As the first few days of the invasion unfolded and James received news of his nemesis' progress, it must have been a relief to find out that there were no more reinforcements coming from his son-in-law and daughter to help their cousin in his invasion. This in turn meant that the king was able to secure London.

As London was being reinforced, Monmouth's rebellion was starting to gather pace. The duke's next move was to head towards the town of Axminister. By this point he had managed to gather an estimated volunteer army of approximately 6,000 Protestant dissenter men, all willing to risk their lives for the duke in order to save the nation from the threat of Rome. From Axminster, Monmouth moved his men to Taunton, a Whig stronghold, and Monmouth found that he was welcomed to the town like a king.

Another reason that Monmouth was able to recruit men within this part of England was that the towns he visited, particularly Axminister, Taunton and Frome, were textile and mining communities, who were in economic recession. The young, unemployed men were frustrated and needed something or someone to blame for their ill fortune and bad circumstances. The rebellion gave these men the prospect to earn money and the fighting offered an opportunity to vent their frustration. It is worth noting that unemployed does not necessarily mean peasant. The records of the trials that would become known as the Bloody Assizes, show that the men who took part in the rebellion were skilled artisans and merchants, such as weavers, tailors, cobblers, blacksmiths, brewers and yeoman farmers. What the men did not have, however, was any formal military training or experience.[67]

When the duke arrived at Taunton on 20 June, there was now no going back on what he had started. The ships that had brought him to his fate had been taken over by the Royal Navy, from where they had been anchored, just off the coast of Lyme Regis. Escape was unfeasible; Monmouth had to give this all he had because he knew what the cost would be if he lost. In Taunton, on 21 June 1685, the Duke of Monmouth was declared King Monmouth by the locals and it is thought that up to 7,000 men had joined his cause by this time.

The next target for 'King Monmouth' was the city of Bristol. If he could capture the city, he would become a serious threat to his rival James II. The king, however, had predicted this next military manoeuvre and on 17 June, while Monmouth was still near the south coast, James sent orders to the Duke of Beaufort, instructing him to lead the local militias of Hereford, Monmouthshire and Gloucester into the city of Bristol to reinforce the city's security. This was very similar to how James had secured the capital against attack. Monmouth's advance towards Bristol was also hampered by heavy rainfall, which unfortunately held up the rebels' progress towards the city. Some historians believe that had Monmouth not been delayed by the weather, he may have had a chance of capturing Bristol before the king.

The Monmouth army then faced problems crossing the River Avon in order to reach Bristol. The problems were due to James' troops and the local militia either destroying or heavily guarding the remaining crossings of the river. Bristol was now no longer an option for Monmouth and so he decided to turn his attention to Bath. This meant edging away from the encroaching Royal forces and moving along the south bank of the River Avon. As they advanced towards Bath, Monmouth sent a messenger ahead of him to demand that the people of the town surrender to him. Bath answered the duke with a clear answer; they shot the messenger and sent him back to Monmouth. The people of Bath were loyal to King James.

This was a disappointing low and it was about to get worse. Monmouth and his men had no choice but to head towards the Somerset town of Frome and it was while Monmouth was encamped there, as his army was slowly depleting, that he heard of the defeat of his comrade, the Earl of Argyll and his subsequent execution. Just when the duke needed some good news, Monmouth's morale was brought lower.

Monmouth had little option but to keep going. His men would find themselves cut off at Trowbridge by a unit of Royalist troops. This meant that the remaining men loyal to Monmouth had to head towards the cathedral city of Wells. The rebels were now low on ammunition and this meant that they had to resort to plundering the west exterior of the cathedral for lead to make more bullets. They further desecrated the building by using the central nave as a stable for their weary horses and animals. From the desecrated cathedral of Wells, the rebels went to the town of Bridgwater; this would be the last stop before what would be the first and final battle of the rebellion that bore Monmouth's name.

On the evening of 5 July 1685, after twenty-five days roaming around the West Country, the Duke of Monmouth and his ragtag army found themselves back in the town of Bridgwater. The rebels were perilously close to the king's men, who were near the plains of Sedgemoor. The king's infantry was led by John Churchill, the future Duke of Marlborough and the men were encamped in a small village called Westernzoyland, located on the edge of the battle site of Sedgemoor.

> Letters from the west inform that on the 6th the late Duke of Monmouth drew his army out of the town of Bridgwater and by a very silent march advanced near his majesties forces…
> the King's forces were about 2000 foot and 700 horse; the rebels were between 5 and 6000 foot and 1200 horses led by the late Lord Grey.[68]

It is not clear where these figures are from, or even whether the numbers are correct. It is worth noting, however, that Monmouth's men were ill-prepared for what they were about to face. Nothing they had encountered thus far on their travels around the west would have prepared them for what was about to happen at Sedgemoor. As well as being ill-prepared and untrained, many of these men were weary after days of marching. The volunteers were armed with little more than pitchforks and farming implements, while those with proper weapons had older fire arms dating from the Civil Wars, as well as basic pikes. They had little reserves and supplies and the majority of their ammunition was what they had hastily made from the lead roofing at Wells Cathedral. On that fateful summer evening of 5 July 1685, Monmouth, along with his officers, including Lord Grey, climbed the church tower of St Mary's in Bridgwater to survey the enemy and plan their attack.

Monmouth knew that he stood the best chance if he attacked by night. So, early on Monday, 6 July, Monmouth led his men to Sedgemoor where the king's troops were encamped. The route that Monmouth's men took started from Bridgwater towards the road to Glastonbury. About half a mile before reaching the said road, the duke's men turned off onto moorland, aided by the cover of darkness. Visibility for these untrained men was poor due to moor fog, which in turn made it difficult to cross the marshy terrain. Through luck more than anything else, Monmouth's men managed to get several miles without detection by the royal forces. They managed to cross the Longmoor Rhyne, a drainage ditch across Sedgemoor that had been dug to help irrigate the plain and avoid flooding, and which was roughly a mile from the site of the battle. As the last of the men and horses crossed the water way, a pistol was accidentally let off. Although it is not clear exactly what happened, the rebel horses, unused to the sound of gun fire, reacted to the fire arm's noise. The rebels had lost their element of surprise.

The poor farm horses that had been commandeered for the rebellion, turned out to be useless in the event of battle; the noise of the fighting soon caused the poor beasts to flee in terror with or without their riders. Now that surprise was no longer on their side, the rebels had no choice but to go in and start fighting. Grey led the remaining mounted men towards the king's cavalry, but it was already clear at this early stage of the battle that the lack of training, organisation and discipline among the volunteer rebel army would be Monmouth's Achilles' heel.

The rebel musketeers and pikemen also had the disadvantage of using old weapons, which would only have been effective had the men organised themselves into a uniformed and strategic formation. Unfortunately, Monmouth's orders were lost within the mêlée as terrified rebels experienced their first proper battle.

The opening stages of the battle were fought during the early hours of the day, when the dawn and foggy mists were still yet to fully break. Both sides tried to recognise their enemy by asking who they were fighting for, and the the rebels cried out in response, 'King Monmouth! King Monmouth!' and 'God with Us!'. The latter being the battle cry used by the Cromwellian parliamentary forces during the Civil Wars.

The lack of trained troops and poor weaponry also hampered Monmouth in battle and the remaining loyal men soon ran out of ammunition.[69] Churchill had trained militia on his side, as well as a good supply of ammunition and weapons. The battle was finally brought to an end when the king's men fired a cannon at Monmouth's followers. Those not killed by the weapon's blast ran in fear of it and fled for their lives. The Battle of Sedgemoor had lasted little over ninety minutes. The rebellion was over. Monmouth's gamble had not paid off and he was now a wanted traitor and on the run from the man he had tried to depose.

Going into the Battle of Sedgemoor, Monmouth was thought to have had 4,000 volunteers; 1,000 more than the royal opposition. An hour and a half of bloody fighting would leave 1,300 of Monmouth's men dead compared to only 200 royal losses. The lack of trained and experienced men, weapons, supplies and discipline would eventually work against the duke's attempt to preserve the Protestant faith and reform the way Britain was governed. Unfortunately, for Monmouth's men, the death toll did not stop after the battle, and a further 320 men would face execution for their treason, including Monmouth himself, while another 750 would be transported for hard labour.

Upon hearing the news of Monmouth's defeat, the Dean of Wells Cathedral is recorded saying:

> The intervening 6 July, auspicious day! Brought an end to the rebellion and downfall to the rebels at Weston Zoyland in this county![70]

There is little wonder that the Dean of the cathedral was happy upon hearing of Monmouth's defeat. If this was the response from a man of the cloth, the Duke of Monmouth could hardly expect compassion from an uncle that he had plotted against. If the duke could not manage to escape to Europe, he must have known that only one fate awaited him.

Monmouth, along with his friend and fellow commander, Lord Grey, now found themselves fleeing for their lives. They changed their clothes for those favoured by peasant farmers in the hope that this would disguise them on the road. Their plan was to reach the coastal town of Poole, Dorset. From there, the pair hoped to catch a ship towards mainland Europe. In an attempt to avoid capture, after two nights on the run and sleeping rough in ditches and hedgerows, the two friends separated in the evening of 7 July. Lord Grey was the first of the two to be discovered and detained, after being found in the New Forest town of Ringwood, in Dorset. The following day the Duke of Monmouth was discovered sleeping in a hedge, wearing provincial clothing. Immediately after the two men's arrest, the *London Gazette* published the following royal proclamation:

> His Majesty has been pleased to cause his Royal Proclaimation to be published for a solemn and publick thanksgiving throughout the kingdom for his majesties late victories over the rebels.[71]

The two friends, Monmouth and Grey, were reunited when they were held for two nights in Ringwood before being brought to London to await their different fates. Monmouth only made one request at Ringwood; he asked to be given paper, pen and ink.

The journey from Dorset to London took four days. The convoy accompanying the rebel leaders was heavily guarded, in order to prevent Whig fanatics from attempting to rescue Monmouth and Grey. During the journey, Monmouth's mood was said to have been melancholic. In comparison, Grey was said to have been positive about the situation they found themselves in:

> The 13 the late Duke of Monmounth and Lord Gray were brought up to town guarded by several troops of horse: the former seem'd much dejected, the latter very cheerful, talking of dogs, hunting, racing and co. They were both sent to the Tower that evening by water, thousands of people being spectators, who seem'd much troubled.[72]

On 13 July, a week after they were defeated at Sedgemoor, the two men reached London. Upon their arrival, the prisoners were transferred from their guarded carriage to waiting barges and taken directly to the Palace of Whitehall to await an audience with King James II and to discover their fates.

Even before the Duke of Monmouth arrived in London, King James had started arranging his rebellious nephew's execution. On 12 July he sent the following memorandum to Lord Guildford, the keeper of the Great Seal to prepare for the event:

> James late Duke of Monmouth, has been attainted by an Act of Parliament made in this present parliament … and thereupon stands attained of high treason and is to suffer the pains of death

as a traitor, which is to be drawn, hanged and quartered; that the said late Duke is now a prisoner at the King's will and pleasure; and that the King is minded to have the manner of this execution changed for certain considerations and causes him especially moved - to make writ to the Lieutenant of the Tower of London or his deputy commanding him forthwith to bring the said late Duke to the accustomed place without the Tower gate and there deliver him to the sheriffs of London .... Commanding them to receive the body of the said late Duke and forthwith to cause execution of him to be done in manner and form following that is to say, forthwith to bring him to the scaffold upon the Tower Hill and then there cause his head to be cut and stricken off clearly severed from his body and this execution to be on Wednesday next the 15 inst., any former judgement law or commandment to the contrary notwithstanding.[73]

James did grant Monmouth an audience, but as can be seen above, the outcome of that meeting was unlikely to have changed, regardless of what Monmouth tried to do in order to save his life. The meeting was probably primarily agreed so that James could give the duke his sentence in person. It is also not unreasonable to assume that the king would have wanted to gloat to his nephew that he was the victor, or even see his nephew beg for mercy, just for pleasure; James II was a vain, petty, frivolous, mean man and such behaviour would not have been beneath him.

Monmouth did not legally require a trial for his part in the rebellion, as parliament had already passed an Act of Attainder. The attainder declared that the Duke of Monmouth was guilty of high treason, nothing therefore could have saved his life, except a royal pardon.

The exchange between uncle and nephew is briefly mentioned within the Calendar of State Papers, but it does not give the details of the conversation or what passed between the two men. What happened in Whitehall stayed in Whitehall. The only source of the meeting was recorded by Sir John Dalrymple in his memoir:

The Duke of Monmouth seemed more concerned and desirous to live and did behave himself not so well as I expected nor so as one ought to have expected from one who had taken upon him to be King. I have signed his death warrant for his execution to-morrow.[74]

Reading that extract, one can only imagine what, in a last-ditch attempt to save himself, Monmouth may have done in the presence of James, maybe even throwing himself at his feet the way he had done with his father after the Rye House Plot. Monmouth was never particularly good at thinking about the consequences of his actions and had always had his father to bail him out of whatever trouble he had got himself into; he had not learned his lesson and now he had run out of luck.

The Duke of Monmouth was left to consider his fate in the Tower of London. James was not completely hard-hearted, as he did allow Monmouth and Grey a few concessions:

> The King ... directs me to tell you that he allows the late Duke of Monmouth and the late Lord Grey should each have a servant but to be shut up with them; that the Bishop of Ely will acquaint the late Duke of Monmouth he is to die to-morrow and that if he desires to see his children it may be allowed, they going with the Bishop of Ely and coming away with him.[75]

Anne, the duke's long-suffering wife, and his neglected children came to visit him in the Tower on the morning of his execution. The duchess' behaviour was very gracious, especially considering his appalling behaviour towards her as her husband. During her visit she asked for his forgiveness and he begged her pardon in return before turning to his children to say his final goodbye.

The Duke of Monmouth was the son of a Stuart monarch and like others before him, found himself facing the executioner instead of growing old and dying in his bed. Some say that he was just another victim of the 'Stuart curse'. However, it may be that he was just unfortunate to live during a particular time of social, political and religious change, and found himself making the wrong decisions with disastrous consequences.

At 10 am on 15 July 1685, the Duke of Monmouth left the prison of the Tower of London and was taken to the gates of the notorious fortress. From there, the Keeper of the Tower handed the duke over to the Sheriffs of London who took him the short distance to the scaffold especially erected on Tower Hill. Unfortunately for Monmouth, his executioner was the infamous Jack Ketch, the notoriously bad executioner, who had so ineptly dispatched Monmouth's friend Lord Russell, at Lincoln's Inn Fields on 21 July 1683.

While in the Tower awaiting his fate, Monmouth had set about putting his affairs in order. He saw his wife and children, but his main worry during his last days and hours seems to have been for the reputation and welfare of his true love, Henrietta Maria, Baroness of Wentworth. Even on the scaffold before dying, Monmouth wanted to try and restore Henrietta's reputation only moments before he took his leave of the world. On the morning of his death, Monmouth is reported to have said the following to Dr Ken, who would later become Bishop of Bath and Wells:

> I confess I lived many years by all sorts of debauchery. But Since that time I had an affection for the Lady Harriot [Henrietta] and I prayed that if were pleasing to God, it might continue, otherwise that it might cease. And God heard my prayer. The affection did continue, therefore I doubted not that it was pleasing to God; and that this is a marriage, our choice of one another being guided, not by lust, but by judgment upon due consideration.[76]

These words are not only well thought out and considered, but are also a tragic yet beautiful declaration of love for a woman who had been so important to Monmouth in the later part of his life. How many of us would be able to think of another like that knowing that we were about to die in such circumstances?

There is further evidence to say that Lady Henrietta was the last person Monmouth thought of as he endured one of the most botched executions of the age. The official record of his execution provides details of the speech he gave before Jack Ketch carried out his grisly business. The established etiquette, for want of a better word, on the scaffold ahead of an execution consisted of a blessing and prayers for the commended, and a speech detailing guilt or innocence, followed by forgiveness to the executioner for doing his job and blessings to the monarch. Until the end, Monmouth was his own man and he used this time to try and restore the honour of his beloved Henrietta Maria, as can be seen by the following conversation, which supposedly took place upon the scaffold:

> **Monmouth:** I have had a scandal raised upon me about a woman, a lady of virtue and honour. I will name her, the lady Henrietta Wentworth. I declare that she is a very virtuous and Godly woman. I have committed no sin with her; and that which hath passed betwixt Us was very Honest and Innocent in the sight of God.

Clerical Assistant: In your opinion perhaps, Sir, as you have been often told; but this is not a fit discourse in this Place.

Mr Sherif: Sir were you ever married to her?

Monmouth: This is not the time to answer that Question.[77]

The Duke of Monmouth's death was also recorded in the following extract taken from Narcissus Luttrell's history of the period:

> The late Duke of Monmouth on the 15, he was accordingly that day brought from the Tower to a scaffold on Tower Hill accompanied by the Bishops of Ely and Bath and Wells, Dr Cartwright, Dean of Rippon and Dr Tension. He was habited in a grey cloth suit...he gave a paper to the Bishops and declared himself for the Church of England: he was very composed. After near an hour he laid himself down and the executioner did his office, but had five blows before he sever'd his head...there was no shouting but many cried: this done his body and head were put into a coffin covered in velvet and carried back to the Tower where after were buried.[78]

In a letter to his son-in-law, William of Orange, King James said that 'He died resolutely and a downright enthusiast.'[79] James' bitterness toward Monmouth is even evident after his nephew's violent and botched execution. Monmouth's death was also recorded in the diary of John Evelyn in the following words, 'darling of his father and the ladies ... debauch'd by lusts, seduc'd by crafty knaves... he failed and perished.'[80] Evelyn's words nicely sum up how many people feel about James Scott, Duke of Monmouth. He ended up on the block because he was spoiled and easily led, but well loved; a duke who tried and failed to win the throne of England.

Traditionally, the bodies of traitors executed for High Treason, either by hanging, drawing and quartering or by beheading, were tarred and left on display on London Bridge as a warning to discourage any other potential traitors. However, James spared his nephew this final humiliation, most probably for the sake of his late brother, rather than for Monmouth himself. The following, taken from the State Papers says:

> July 14 Earl of Sunderland to the sheriffs of London. I have acquainted the King with what you desire me, upon which his

Majesty directs me to tell you that he allows the scaffold for
the execution of the late Duke of Monmouth should be covered
with mourning, and that his body after execution be given to
his friends to be disposed of as they shall see fit.[81]

James Scot, former Duke of Monmouth, was laid to rest in the Tower of
London's chapel of St Peter ad Vincula. He still lies in that chapel, resting
for all eternity, in a grave situated under the altar.

Epilogue

The execution of the Duke of Monmouth upon Tower Hill did not bring an end to the punishment and retribution for the many men who joined him in his rebellion. Those who were hardest hit by the full force of the law during the late summer of 1685 were the poor Protestant farmers and traders who had joined with the duke in the West Country. Due to the severity of the offence committed by the rebels, James II used the full force of the English law to hunt down those involved and punish them as a message to the rest of the nation - the message was clear; he was king and he would not tolerate rebellion.

King James' first action was to commission an Oyer and Terminer to his Lord Chief Justice. This was to ensure that the rebels currently held within the West Country gaols would be tried and punished at the soonest possible opportunity. Those who had been imprisoned shortly after the end of the rebellion, found themselves crammed into small cells in the summer heat. Many had acquired injuries at the Battle of Sedgemoor and with poor food and hygiene levels being non-existent, as expected from a seventeenth-century gaol, a good number of these poor men contracted and succumbed to what was known as 'gaol fever' (typhus), while waiting for the assizes to start. Some may say these men were the lucky ones.

The start of the trials, which would become known as the Bloody Assizes, were delayed as the now infamous Lord Chief Justice, Judge Jeffreys, had been suffering from painful kidney stones. Eventually the Assize session started eleven days after Monmouth's death, on 26 July 1685, in Winchester. Scores of men came in front of the Justice and fellow judges and the majority were found guilty of high treason for their involvement in the rebellion. Of those who were found guilty, 250 were eventually executed and a further 750 were transported for ten years hard labour in the West Indies. One of the lucky ones was Daniel Foe, who would later write the novel *Robinson Crusoe* (published under the name Daniel Defoe). According to some, the story was based on the life of Dr Harry Pittman, who ended up as a bonded servant to a Barbados plantation owner.

The effect on the communities of the West Country who witnessed this number of men hanging from gallows and seeing the corpses of hung, drawn and quartered men on display, must have been tremendously traumatic. Little mercy was given to those who faced the noose, as Jack Ketch, who had literally butchered the Duke of Monmouth's execution, was brought down to the west, in order to help carry out these sentences.

James II's behaviour in the aftermath of the rebellion, did nothing to alleviate the people's fear of his reign. All that he did was to confirm the nation's fears about how the Catholic monarch would behave towards his Protestant subjects, serving only to increase their fear, distrust and the national anxiety towards him.

Lord Grey, who had been arrested with Monmouth in Dorset and who subsequently travelled to London with his friend, managed to escape the same fate as the duke. Grey freely turned king's informer and betrayed his former allies and comrades in exchange for his life. Despite his stint as a traitor and rebel, Grey would turn his life around under the reign of William III, when he rose through the political ranks, first to Privy Councillor, then Lord Treasurer, to Lord Chief Justice and finally Lord Privy Seal; a post he still held at the time of his death, in 1701.

Another of the prominent rebels who escaped capture and conviction was Robert Ferguson, who managed to flee to the coast and find passage back to the Low Countries, following the defeat at Sedgemoor. He would stay in northern Europe until returning to England with William III in 1689. This association did not last long. William was wary of Ferguson and the Scot was never part of the new king's inner circle. Ferguson saw this as an insulting and personal snub, which in turn caused this angry former rebel to start communicating with leading Jacobites, who ironically supported the now exiled James II. Unsurprisingly, the Jacobites, like William III, also failed to take Ferguson seriously. The angry Scot somehow evaded trial for his treasonous pamphlets against the new king and government and died angry, embittered and in poverty in 1714.

There were two women who also lost their lives as a result of the Bloody Assizes. Their crimes were for harbouring and aiding known rebels. Both these women came from opposite ends of the social scale. The first was Lady Alice Lisle, who had been married to former republican MP John Lisle. Her crime was to offer shelter to two men, John Hicks and Richard Nelthorpe on 28 July 1685. Both men were said to have fought for the Duke of Monmouth at the Battle of Sedgemoor. As a member of the gentry she was shown the mercy of being beheaded, rather than hanged or burned at the stake. She died at Winchester on 2 September 1685 aged 71 years old, and has an engraved headstone in the Parish church of Ellingham, St Mary and & All Saints.

The second woman was Elizabeth Gaunt, a poor Anabaptist, who would be the last woman to be executed for the political crime of treason in England. Sadly, her fate was not as merciful as Lady Lisle's. Her crime was to have helped James Burton escape to Europe in 1683, after the discovery of the Rye House Plot. When he was subsequently arrested for his involvement with the Monmouth Rebellion in 1685, the coward turned king's informer and implicated Elizabeth in order to save his own neck. Consequently, she was tried and sentenced at the Old Bailey. Her sentence was to die being burned at the stake. On 19 October 1685, Elizabeth was brought to the stake and reportedly picked up one of the faggots 'and kissed it' saying 'it was of little consideration to her whether she died in the fire' or 'in her bed.' Her death was witnessed by William Penn, who would go on to establish the colony of Pennsylvania in America.

Famously, in 1768, the French writer and playwright, Germain-Francois Poullain de Saint-Foix, stated that the Duke of Monmouth had in fact escaped the axe on Tower Hill and that another poor soul was executed in his place. He went on to claim that Monmouth was the infamous 'Man in the Iron Mask'. The reason De Saint-Foix gave for this was that King James had no stomach for executing his own nephew. Of all the myths and rumours surrounding James Duke of Monmouth, especially those after his death, this is the least likely to be true.

Although James Scott, Duke of Monmouth and Buccleuch, Earl of Doncaster, Dalkeith, Scott of Tindale, Whitchester and Ashdale was the illegitimate issue of Charles II, his life and role within seventeenth-century British history played an important part in creating our modern nation.

Monmouth lived during a time of major readjustment politically, socially and religiously in a post Restoration Britain. Political parties were starting to develop, the monarch's role was struggling to be redefined in a post republican era, the roles of the state and church were endeavouring to find where they should be in relation to each other.

Men such as Shaftesbury and his fellow Exclusionists saw the Duke of Monmouth as a malleable political solution to exclude the Catholic York from the throne. In contrast, Monmouth saw these men as allies and friends. In this situation, Monmouth was always going to be callously used by these men who manipulated him and saw him as disposable; the duke was just a tool to help further their own political goals and ambitions. Signs of this were evident after the exposure of the Rye House Plot in 1683. There is little to no evidence that Monmouth knew the full treasonous details of the plot, but the main plotters ensured he was implicated enough that should the plot have succeeded, Monmouth would have been willing and agreeable to help them.

Had Monmouth succeeded in his rebellion would he have made a good king? In all honesty, Monmouth probably would not have been a good choice of monarch; he had too many of the bad qualities of his father, namely his libertine and pleasure seeking lifestyle and desire to please everyone, which he believed was easier than standing up and doing the right thing. However, had Monmouth been crowned, his reign would most likely have been different to that of his father's. Firstly, he would have been in a dangerous situation and been forced to find a way to work with parliament, otherwise he would have undoubtedly found himself being removed by the government. If the rebellion had been victorious; it would also have probably thrown the nation back into a protracted civil war. If James II had survived the rebellion, his personality suggests that he would have persuaded his nephew to be merciful and fought to regain his throne. With hindsight, either outcome of the rebellion shows that an insurrection against James II, so soon after the death of his brother, Charles II, would not have brought an easy, peaceful or lasting solution to the nation's problems of religion, succession and the role of state and monarch within Britain at this time.

Had the Duke of Monmouth waited until the inevitable time when his uncle James had managed to alienate his parliament and country, it is unlikely that the government would have invited him, rather than William and Mary, to rule Britain, mainly on the grounds of his illegitimate status. However, he would have at least been alive and would probably have held a prominent position within the royal court of his cousins. Of course, this is all speculation aided by hindsight; going to show that Monmouth was rash and wrong to attempt an insurrection when he did.

The legacy of the rise and fall of the Duke of Monmouth can be seen in the Glorious Revolution of 1688. It had become clear that James II had to go, but parliament forced this change using the law, rather than on the battlefield, as Monmouth had tried to do. With this new dawn, the monarchy's role changed from ruler to figurehead, becoming more like the democratic political system we use today. This was the same system of government that started to germinate during the reign of Charles II. The Duke of Monmouth had been one the catalysts to start this process in the early 1680s, thus forming part of the legacy he left us.

EPILOGUE

In the subsequent reigns of William and Mary and of tragic Queen Anne, the Stuart line would end its rule in Britain. With the need of an heir once again an issue of importance, parliament introduced the Act of Settlement in 1701. Although Anne had seventeen pregnancies and five live births, none of her children lived beyond the age of eleven, this being Prince William, Duke of Gloucester. When it became clear that she was unlikely to have an heir, the Act of Settlement was passed to prevent the issue of 'exclusion' over religious background from resurfacing as it did in the 1680s.

Upon his execution, the Dukedom of Monmouth ended and has not been resurrected since. The other titles James Scott held, including the Dukedom of Buccleuch, were those he gained by marriage and were thus unaffected by his execution. These titles returned to his heirs through his grandson, Francis Scott, who was made Duke of Buccleuch upon the death of his grandmother, the former Duchess of Monmouth.

Considering that Monmouth's marriage was one of convenience and not love, he and the duchess did conceive six children, the last of whom was born in 1683. Only two of these legitimate children would survive into adulthood. The first was James Scott, Earl of Dalkeith (1674-1705), who married into the Hyde family and with his wife Henrietta Hyde (daughter of the poet the first Earl of Rochester), were the parents of Francis Scott, who would go on to inherit Monmouth's title of Duke of Buccleuch.

The second child was Henry Scott, First Earl of Deloraine (1676-1730), who served Queen Anne as an elected member of her Scottish Parliament. He would also help pass the the Act of Union in 1707 by voting in its favour. The title survives and the 10th and current Duke of Buccleuch is Richard Walter John Montagu Douglas Scott. He is also the 12th Duke of Queensbury.

James Scott, Duke of Monmouth, was a man of his time; he embodied the Restoration period, through his family, politics, religion, lifestyle, friends, enemies and even his death. He lived his life fully, loved passionately and fought bravely, whether legally or rebelliously. He lived in a period of great events and was at the centre of a political crisis. His mark on history should be of a man who was complex, brave, handsome, charming, loyal and naive, rather than as a rebel, criminal and victim, and who embodied seventeenth-century Britain at its best, as well as its worst.

Appendix

Monmouth in 17th Century and Contemporary Literature

Even during his lifetime, the Duke of Monmouth did not escape the popular satirical culture of the seventeenth century. The two satirical writers most associated with depicting the Duke of Monmouth were John Dryden, the first Poet Laureate, and Aphra Behn, a pioneering female writer and playwright. Dryden and Behn were on opposite sides of support for the duke during the Exclusion Crisis, as well as being on opposing sides of the fledgling political party system. These political leanings are reflected within their works and through the people they were associated with during their lifetimes.

John Dryden – Absalom and Achitophel

The John Dryden work most associated with the Duke of Monmouth is *Absalom and Achitophel*, which uses an Old Testament biblical narrative to reflect the politics of the day, but most especially that of the Exclusion Crisis led by the Earl of Shaftesbury, and features Monmouth's relationship with his father and York. The seventeenth-century audience would have automatically understood the comparisons between the Old Testament story and who each of the characters represented in this witty, observant, politically aware piece of poetry.

The main biblical characters in the poem represent the following historical characters:

> King David – Charles II
> Absalom, King David's cherished and adored son – the Duke of Monmouth
> Achitophel, King David's advisor – the Earl of Shaftesbury
> Israel – London
> Egyptian religion – French religion (Catholicism)

In the Old Testament story, Absalom was King David's favourite son and is described as being handsome and charming, with a love for the pomp and splendour of the royal court and beloved by his father's people. All is well until Absalom falls out of favour with his father, after the former killed his half brother and the heir to the throne, Amnon. After being estranged for three years, Absalom eventually came back into his father's favour and upon their reconciliation, the people of Jerusalem regarded Absalom as the new heir to the throne.

Absalom encouraged the popular support and, four years later, was persuaded by his 'friend' Achitophel to seize the throne from his father, King David and declare himself king. The two forces came together for the climatic battle of Ephraim Woods, which resulted in Absalom fleeing for his life. He was eventually found three days later after his hair had become caught in the branches of an oak tree. In spite of David's explicit command not to harm him, Absalom was killed by three darts to the heart.

The poem in itself is prophetic in that Absalom did indeed rebel to remove his father, but was forgiven; at the time of publication, this could have been seen to reflect the events surrounding the Rye House Plot, after which Monmouth was publicly forgiven for his possible involvement. However, Monmouth did then carry out a rebellion in his name to overthrow the king. Unlike the biblical story, his uncle, King James II, had no great love for his nephew and this time he was not forgiven.

The following extract is the opening of Absalom and Achitophel:

> When Man, on many, multiply'd his kind,
> E'r one to one was cursedly, confin'd:
> When nature prompted, and no law deny'd,
> Promiscuous use of Concubine and Bride;
> Then, Israel's monarch, after Heaven's own heart,
> His vigorous warmth did, variously, impart
> To Wives and Slaves; And, wide as his command,
> Scattered his Maker's Image through the Land.
> Michal, of Royal blood, the Crown did wear,
> A Soil ungrateful to the Tiller's care;
> Not so the rest; for several Mothers bore
> To Godlike David, several Sons before.
> But since like slaves his bed they did ascend,
> No True Succession could their seed attend.
> Of all this Numerous Progeny was none
> so beautiful, so brave as Absalom.

The poem is not critical of the Duke of Monmouth, but of the Earl of Shaftesbury and his Exclusionists and how they used Monmouth for their own political gain. Although Monmouth as Absalom was at the centre of the poem, he was the victim of others' ambitions and circumstances of the time, both politically and religiously, rather than due to his own personal gain; therefore Dryden is critical of the Exclusionists rather than of Monmouth.

Aphra Behn – Love Letters Between a Nobleman and His Sister

Aphra Behn was a child of the Civil Wars and it is thought that she spent part of the Commonwealth years living in Surinam, returning to Britain in the early years of Charles II's Restoration, before possibly working as a spy for the crown. While her religious beliefs remain unknown, the company she kept and her support for the Duke of York suggests that she was Catholic, rather than Anglican. She was one of the first English women to earn a living from writing and upon her death had composed nineteen plays, as well as a catalogue of poetry and other works. She died on 16 April 1689, having, in her own words, lived her life 'dedicated to pleasure and poetry'.

The Aphra Behn work that is connected with Monmouth is entitled *Love Letters Between A Nobleman And His Sister* and was published in three parts over a period of four years from 1684-1688. Initially, the work aimed to satirise one of Monmouth's friends, Ford Grey, 1st Earl of Tankerville and his notorious, passionate and scandalous affair with his sister in law, Lady Henrietta Berkeley. It is the third volume of the work that concerns the Monmouth Rebellion, with the Duke of Monmouth represented by the character Cesario, who has presumptive ambitions to become the king of France. Monmouth's last mistress and true love, Lady Henrietta Maria Wentworth, is also represented in the story by the character Hermione.

In Behn's work, the doomed anti-hero Cesario sets out from Brussels in pursuit of becoming the king of France through rebellion. Behn portrays the character of Cesario as gullible, easily lead and deluded in the belief that his scheme to become king will succeed. The story's end also mirrors the outcome of the real Monmouth's rebellion; Cesario is defeated by the French king's army and executed for his treasonous rebellion against the crown. It would have been clear to contemporary audiences that Behn was, in fact, depicting Monmouth's Rebellion. Had Behn been pro-Monmouth, she could have easily amended the end of the story to depict a Utopian new France under Cesario's rule, but instead, she championed the Catholic French king.

The following works of fiction also feature the Duke of Monmouth, either as a central or incidental character, or are set during the time of the Monmouth Rebellion:

Old Mortality, Sir Walter Scott (1816)
Lorna Doone, R. D. Blackmore (1869)
Micah Clarke, Sir Arthur Conan Doyle (1889)
Martin Hyde, John Masefield (1921)
Captain Blood, Rafael Sabatini (1922)
Lillibullero, Robert Neill (1975)
The Royal Changeling, John Whitbourn (1998)
Tamsin, Peter S. Beagle (1999)
His Rebel Bride, Helen Dickinson (2003)
The Monmouth Summer, Tim Vicary (2011)
His Last Mistress, Andrea Zuvich (2013)
A Want of Kindness, Joanne Limburg (2015)

Bibliography

Primary Sources
Newspapers & Pamphlets
London Gazette (1660-1685)

Anon., *An Account of what passed at the Execution of the late Duke of Monmouth* (London: 1685)

Crown, George, *A Copy of the Late Duke of Monmouth's letter to the Duke of Albemarle* (London: 1685)

Harris, Benjamin, *His Grace the Duke of Monmouth Honoured in his Progress in the West of England in An Account of a Most Extraordinary Cure of the Kings Evil* (London: 1680)

State Papers, Manuscripts & Registers
Historical Manuscripts Commission
Calendar of State Papers Domestic series dating from 1600-1686 (London, Longman & Co: 1860)

Calendar of State Papers Domestic series dating from Feb-Dec 1685 (London: 1960)

The Manuscripts of the most Honourable Marquis of Ormonde preserved at the Castle Kilkenny (London: 1895)

Calendar of Manuscripts of the Marquis of Bath, Volume 1 (London: 1904)

Calendar of the Manuscripts of the Dean and Chapter of Wells, Volume 2 (London: 1907-1914)

Report on the Manuscripts of the Duke of Buccleuch and Queensbury Preserved at Montague House, Volume 1 (London: 1899)

Macray, Rev William Dunn (Ed.), *Calendar of Clarendon State Papers in the Bodleian Library,* Vol 3 1655-1657 (Oxford, Clarendon Press: 1872)

Rouledge, F J (Ed.), *Calendar of Clarendon State Papers in the Bodleian Library,* Vol 4 1657-1660 (Oxford, Clarendon Press: 1872)

The Register of the Privy Council of Scotland, Third Series, Volumes 9 – 11 (Edinburgh: HM General Register House, 1908-1970)

BIBLIOGRAPHY

Diaries, Memoirs, Personal Letters & Volumes of Poetry

Dalrymple, Sir John, *The Memoirs of Great Britain and Ireland from the Dissolution of the Last Parliament of Charles II Until the Sea Battle of La Hogue,* Volumes I & II (London, W. Strahan:1771)

Dryden John, *Absalom and Achitophitel, A Poem* (London, Printed by Jacob Tonson, Sold By W. Davis: 1681)

Duckett, Sir G. (ed.), *Original letters of the Duke of Monmouth in the Bodleian Library* (London: 1879)

Evelyn, John and William Bray (ed.), *The Diary of John Evelyn,* Volumes 1 & 2 (London: 1901)

Luttrell, Narcissus, *A Brief Historical Relation of State Affairs,* Volume 1 (Oxford, Oxford University Press: 1857)

Pepys, Samuel, *The Diary of Samuel Pepys: A Selection* (London, Penguin Classics, 2003)

Pepys, Samuel, *The Great Fire of London* (London, Penguin Little Black Classics, 2015)

Pope, Alexander (ed.), *A Collection of Poems Relating to State Affairs from Oliver Cromwell to this Present Time by the Greatest Wits of the Age* (London: 1705)

Sidney, Colonel H., (afterwards Earl of Romney) 1 June 1679 - 13 Jan 1682 printed in the diary of the times of Charles II (British Library ref: Add MS 32682)

Secondary Sources
Books

Banks, Thomas C., *Baronia Angelica Concentrata* (Ripon: 1844)

Barbary, James, *Puritan and Cavalier* (London, Puffin: 1977)

Bevan., B., *James, Duke of Monmouth* (London, Robert Hale: 1973)

Chandler, David, *Sedgemoor, 1685: An Account and an Anthology* (London, Palgrave Macmillan: 1985)

Clark, Sir George Norman, *The Oxford History of England, The Later Stuarts 1660-1714,* Vol 10 (Oxford, Oxford University Press: 1934)

Clarke, Reverend J. S. (ed.), *The Life of James II (From notes left in his own hand)* Vol 1 (Orme & Brown: 1816)

Earle, Peter, *Monmouth's Rebels: The Road to Sedgemoor 1685* (London, Weidenfeld & Nicolson: 1977)

Frasier, Antonia, *King Charles II* (London, Weilenfeld & Nicolson: 1979)

Greaves, Richard L., *Secrets of the Kingdom, British Radicals from the Popish Plot to the Revolution of 1688-89* (California, Stanford University Press: 1992)

Harris, Tim, *Politics Under The Later Stuarts: Party Conflict in a Divided Society, 1660-1715* (Routledge: 1993)

Harris, Tim, *Restoration: Charles II and his Kingdoms 1660-1685* (London, Penguin: 2006)

Harris, Tim, *Revolution: The Great Crisis of the British Monarchy 1685-1720* (London, Penguin: 2006)

Hutton, Ronald, *Charles II: King of England, Scotland and Ireland* (Clarendon Press: 1989)

Hyde, E., *The Life of Edward, Earl of Clarenden: Selections From The History Of The Rebellion & The Life By Himself* (Oxford University Press: 1978)

Jones, James Rees, *The First Whigs: The Politics of the Exclusion Crisis 1678-1683* (London, Oxford University Press: 1961)

Jones, James Rees, *The Revolution of 1688 in England,* (London, Weilenfeld & Nicolson: 1972)

Keay, Anna, *The Last Royal Rebel: The Life and Death of James, Duke of Monmouth* (London, Bloomsbury: 2016)

Kenyon, John (ed.), *Pelican Classics Halifax Complete Works* (London, Penguin: 1969)

Kenyon, John, *The Popish Plot* (Phoenix: 2000)

Kishlansky, Mark, A *Monarchy Transformed, Britain 1603-1714* (London, Penguin: 1997)

Knights, Mark, *Politics and Opinion in Crisis 1678-81* (Cambridge, Cambridge University Press: 1994)

Lodge, Richard, *The Political History of England 1660-1702,* Vol 8 (New York, AMS Press Kraus Reprint Co.: 1969)

Macaulay, Baron Thomas Babington, *The History of England from the Accession of James II,* Vol 1 (London, Longman Brown: 1858)

McEllingott, Jason (ed.), *Fear, Exclusion & Revolution: Roger Morrice and Britain in the 1680s* (Aldershot, Ashgate Publishing Ltd: 2006)

Miller, John, *Bourbon and Stuart: Kings and Kingship in France and England in the Seventeenth Century* (London, Philip: 1987)

Miller, John, *Charles II* (London, Weidenfeld & Nicolson: 1991)

Miller, John, *An English Absolutism? The Later Stuart Monarchy 1660-88* (London, Historical Association: 1992)

Miller, John, *After the Civil Wars: English Politics and Government in the Reign of Charles II* (New York, Longman: 2000)

Miller, John, *James II* (London, Yale University Press: 2000)

Morrill, John et al, *Reactions to the English Civil War 1642-1649* (Macmillan Press Ltd: 1982)

Nepean, Maud, *On the Left of a Throne: A Personal Study of James Duke of Monmouth* (London, John Lane: 1914)

Roberts, George, *The Life, Progresses and Rebellion of James Duke of Monmouth to his Capture and Execution: With a full account of the Bloody Assize and Copious Biographical Notices,* Volume 1 & 2 (London: 1844)

Smith, David L., *The Stuart Parliaments 1603-1689* (Arnold Publishers: 1999)

Starkey, David, *Elizabeth* (London, Vintage: 2001)

BIBLIOGRAPHY

Tinniswood, Adrian, *By Permission of Heaven: The Story Of The Great Fire Of London* (Pimlico: 2004)

Uglow, Jenny, *A Gambling Man* (Faber and Faber: 2010)

Waller, Maureen, *Ungrateful Daughters: The Stuart Princesses Who Stole Their Father's Throne* (London, Hodder & Stoughton: 2002)

Watson J.N.P., *Captain-General and Rebel Chief: The Life of James Duke of Monmouth* (London, George Allen & Unwin: 1979)

Willock, John, *A Scots Earl in Covenanting Times* (Edinburgh, Andrew Elliot: 1907)

Zook, Melinda., *Protestantism, Politics and Women in Britain, 1660-1714* (London, Palgrave Macmillan: 2013)

Journals

Milne, Doreen J., 'The Results of the Rye House Plot & Their Influence upon the Revolution of 1688: The Alexander Prize Essay', *Transactions of the Royal Historical Society* Vol. 1 (1951), pp. 91-108

Milton, Philip, 'John Locke and the Rye House Plot', *The Historical Journal* Vol. 43 No. 3 (Sep., 2000), pp. 674-668

Online sources

Challoner, Richard, *Memoirs of Missionary Priests and other Catholics of both sexes that have suffered death in England on religious accounts from the year 1577 to 1684* (Manchester, T. Haydock: 1803) Retrieved from http://www.british-history.ac.uk/statutes-realm/vol5/pp782-785

Endnotes

Chapter 1

1 Essex was clearly following the family tradition as his father, the 2nd Earl of Essex, was executed by Elizabeth I in 1601 for high treason.

2 Calendar of State Papers Domestic Series 1641-1643, vol I, Thomas Wiseman to Sir John Pennington, 6 Jan 1642, p.240.

Chapter 2

2 Clarendon Papers, Minutes from a Conversation between Mr Moungo Murray, Hyde and Mr Mowbray 5-7 December 1648, p.459.

3 Macray, Rev William Dunn (ed.), Calendar of the Clarendon State Papers in the Bodleian Library Volume 3, 1655-1657, letter from Don Alonso de Cardenas to the King, 6 Dec, pp.392-3.

4 Ibid., Letter from Ormonde to Mottet, 10 Dec 1657, p.394.

5 Nepean, Maud, *On the Left of a Throne: A Personal Study of James Duke of Monmouth*, p.15.

Chapter 3

6 Evelyn, J, *Diary*, 29 May 1660.

7 Ibid., 29 May 1660.

8 Harris, T., *Politics Under The Later Stuarts*, p.82.

Chapter 4

9 Evelyn, J., *Diary*, 30 May 1662.

10 Pepys, S., *Diary*, 31 May 1662.

Chapter 5

11 Pepys, S., *Diary*, 31 December 1662.

12 Evelyn, J., *Diary*, 18 August 1649.

13 Sydney, H., *Diary*, Vol1, p.263.

14 Monmouth Pocket Book, Egerton MS 1527.

15 HMC, Appx V, to report 12 Vol II (Rutland MS) 84.

16 Comte d'Avaux, Vol III 64-5, 1754.

17 Watson JNP, *Captain General and Rebel Chief, the life of James Duke of Monmouth,* p.204.

18 Banks, T., *Baronia Anglica Concentrata*, p.454

Chapter 6

19 Historical Manuscripts Commission; *Calendar State Papers Domestic series, Ded 1671 - May 1672,* April 29 1672 p.391.

20 Roberts, G., *Life Of The Duke Of Monmouth*, p.34.

21 Evelyn, J., Diary, 21 August 1674.

22 Historical Manuscripts Commission, *The Manuscripts of the most Honourable Marquis of Ormonde* preserved at the Castle Kilkenny New series Vol 5; Letter from Henry Coventry to Ormonde, June 28 1679, (London: 1895) p.146.

23 Bevan, B., *James Duke of Monmouth*, p.105.

Chapter 7

24 Pepys, S., *Diary*, 26 July 1665.

25 Clarke, Rev J.S. (ed.), *The Life of James II (From notes left in his own hand)* Vol 1, 1816, p.567.

26 Thompson, E.M. (ed), Hatton, Correspondence of the family of Hatton 1601-1704 (1878) Vol1 p.194.

27 Dalrymple, Sir John, *Memoirs of Great Britain and Ireland 1790*, Vol I, p.328-9.

28 Pepys, S., *The Great Fire of London*, p.39.

29 Hyde, E., *The Life Of Edward, Earl of Clarendon*, p.291.

30 Kishlansky, M., *A Monarchy Transformed, Britain 1603-1714*, p.257.

Chapter 8

31 Hutton, R., *Charles II*, p.360.

32 Evelyn, J., *Diary*, 6 November 1680.

33 Ormonde Manuscripts at Kilkenny Castle, Vol1 p.25-26.

34 Hutton, R., *Charles II*, p.366.

35 Evelyn, J., *Diary*, 7 December 1680.

Chapter 9

36 Roberts, G., *The Life, Progresses and Rebellion of James Duke of Monmouth*, p.109-10.

37 Calendar of Manuscripts of Duke of Ormonde Vol V, Letter Earl of Ossory to Ormande, December 2 1679.

Chapter 10

38 Historical Manuscript Commission, the manuscript of the most Hon Marquis of Ormond preserved and the castle of Kilkenny, New series Vol 7; Letter Col Cooke to Ormond, 29 November 1679.

39 Harris, B., *His Grace the Duke of Monmouth Honoured in his Progress in the West of England in An Account of a Most Extraordinary Cure of the Kings Evil, 1680*, p.2.

40 Charles II, Oxford Parliament, 28th March 1681.

41 Ibid.

42 Ibid.

Chapter 11

43 Keay A., *The Last Royal Rebel*, p.287.

44 *London Gazette*, 22 - 26 March 1683.

45 Luttrell, N., *A Brief Historical Relation of State Affairs* Vol 1, p.253.

46 Calendar of manuscripts of the Marquess of Ormond, New Series Vol II, p.65.

47 Ibid., Letter between Sir Robert Reading and the Earl of Arran, 8 December 1683, p.165.

48 Ibid., Letter between Sir Robert Reading and the Earl of Arran, 4 December 1683, p.65.

49 Historical Manuscripts Commission; Calendar of State Papers Charles II, Domestic series, October 1st 1683 - April 30, London, Longman & Co: 1860, The depositions of Ezekiel Everest Jan 19, 1684, p. 226.

50 Ibid., Letter from the Duchess of Monmouth to Charles II, 15 October 1683, p.35.

51 Roberts, G., *The Life And Progresses Of James Duke Of Monmouth and His Capture and Execution*, p.160.

52 Historical Manuscripts Commission; Calendar of State Papers Charles II, Domestic series, October 1 1683 - April 30; Letter to Jenkins 30 Nov 1683, p.124.

53 Ibid., Letter to Jenkins 18 March 1684, p.329.

54 Calendar State Papers Domestic series May 1 1684 - Feb 5 1685.

55 Evelyn, J., *Diary*, 4 February 1685.

56 Ibid.

57 Ibid.

58 Bevan, B., *James, Duke of Monmouth*, p.183.

Chapter 12

59 Historical Manuscripts Commission; Calendar of State Papers Domestic series dating from Feb-Dec 1685; London,1960, Entry 138; p.30.

60 The Register of the Privy Council of Scotland, Third Series, Volume 10; Edinburgh. HM General Register House, 1908-1970, p.327.

ENDNOTES

61 Luttrell, N., *A Brief Historical Relation of State Affairs*, p.348.

62 Register of the Privy Council of Scotland, Third series Volume 11, 20 June 1685, p.x.

63 Ibid. p.327.

64 Willock, J., *A Scots Earl in Covenanting Times*, p 421.

65 The Manuscripts of the most Honourable Marquis of Ormond New series Vol 7, p.354.

66 Earle, P., *Monmouth's Rebels: The Road to Sedgemoor 1685*, p.59.

67 Chandler, D., *Sedgemoor 1685*, p.8.

68 Luttrell, N., *A Brief Historical Relation of State Affairs,* p.351.

69 Macaulay, Baron Thomas Babington, *The History of England from the Accession of James II*, Vol 1.

70 Calendar of the Manuscripts of the Dean and Chapter of Wells, Vol 2, p.448.

71 *London Gazette,* 9 – 13 July 1685.

72 Luttrell, N., *A Brief Historical Relation of State Affairs*, p.353.

73 Historical Manuscripts Commission; Calendar of State Papers Domestic series dating from State Papers Domestic, Feb-Dec 1685, p.259.

74 Dalrymple, J., *The Memoirs of Great Britain and Ireland*, p.134.

75 Calendar of State Papers James II, Domestic series, Feb-Dec 1685, Entry 1221, p.261.

76 Eachard L, History of England, Vol I, p.1060.

77 An account of what passed at the execution of the late Duke of Monmouth.

78 Luttrell, N., *A Brief Historical Relation of State Affairs*, p.353-4.

79 Dalrymple, J., *The Memoirs of Great Britain and Ireland*; James' letter to William of Orange, 17 July 1685, p.135.

80 Evelyn, J., *Diary*, 15 July 1685.

81 Historical Manuscripts Commission; Calendar of State Papers Domestic series dating from State Papers Domestic, Feb-Dec 1685, p261.

Index

INDEX